D0369021

Tear in the Desert

A Journey into the Heart of the Iraq War with Navy Chaplain Father Ron Moses Camarda

Father Ron with 3-1 Marines just before returning for home
Col Willy Buhl, USMC is on the far right.

Published by Ron Moses Camarda

Printed in the United States of America

ISBN 978-0-6151-9578-0

Cover photo (L-R) My bodyguard RP1 Patrick Bowen, USNR, the author, Chaplain Dwight Horn and RP3 Demetri Givans.

Edited by Maria Lee Richburg

Read the *Florida Times Union*
story of Father Ron in Iraq online
at www.jacksonville.com
Story title: THE BEST CHRISTMAS EVER
by Mark Woods, Dec 25, 2005

Table of Contents

YAWEH T HEWAY

Introduction

Jesus used stories. This is a book of stories. Part of the book is my story, but it is also the story of how millions of people had their lives changed forever.

This story is everyone's story. All of us are born from a man and a woman. All of us are in need of abundant love and joy and sorrow. We need food and shelter and peace. O yes, we need peace. And this may sound even more incredible…We all need war.

This is a story about journeying into war and coming home to realize that we must be rescued from the war within. The story begins in the desert amidst the mystery and marvel of a single solitary tear. The tear has been tearing me apart and drowning me. The tear will also make me whole and call me to an authentic life.

A very weak and unworthy person tells this story. I tell it with feelings of love and fear, but mostly of love. I am continually transformed and transfigured by this story. I am filled with gratitude beyond all telling for the tear that *is* the story.

I am about to tell this story.
You are about to tell this story.
We are about to tell this story.
I am.

You are.

We are.

The Story.

The Birth.

The Tear in the Desert.

And the Death.

Psalm 55

My heart is stricken within me,
death's ***terror*** *is on me,*
Trembling and fear fall upon me
and horror overwhelms me.

O that I had wings like a dove
to fly away and be at rest.
So I would escape far away
and take refuge in the ***desert.***

I would hasten to find a shelter
from the raging wind,
from the destructive storm, O Lord,
and from their plotting tongues.

For I can see nothing but violence
and strife in the city.
Night and day they patrol
high on the city walls.

It is full of wickedness and evil;
it is full of sin.
Its streets are never free
from tyranny and deceit...

Who will separate us from the love of Christ? Trial, or distress, or persecution, or hunger, or nakedness, or danger, or the sword? Yet in all this we are more than conquerors because of him who has loved us.

– Saint Paul to the Romans 8:35-37

Tear in the Desert is my journey. I share it with all of my idiosyncrasies and biases. I share it with love. I pray and hope you will find comfort in it and not terror or despair. It is probably a story told since the beginning of the human race, whenever that was. I hope we all grow and benefit from tears shared by those who died for a worthy cause, one they believed to be closer to the divine, the spirit of love.

God bless you and thank you for taking this journey. I dedicate this story to your heart and your capacity to love. For without love, there would be no tear.

Chapter I
Dale

14 November 2004

Those who welcome the Word as the guest of their hearts will have abiding joy. But I through the greatness of your love have access to your house.

I was alone in the Chapel Office of Camp Fallujah talking to my brother in New Jersey. Mid conversation, the phone went dead. I hung up and tried again. The line was silent.

I quickly e-mailed my brother so he wouldn't worry. As I clicked to send the message, the phone rang. Patrick, my RP1 (Religious Program Specialist and Protector), was calling from Bravo Surgical 200 yards away. Someone was dying who was most likely Catholic. So off I went, oblivious to the angels around me. I entered the operating room. I could smell death.

Dale, a typical Marine, tattooed and somewhat hardened, was there before me on a gurney. He had suffered a gunshot wound to the head, the work of a cowardly and desperate sniper. Dale was, as they say, *expectant.* His breathing was strong, although it was rapidly slowing down. I had often observed this situation with Hospice and the dying. Strange as it seems, I knew Dale was waiting for me. Often, the clothes of the injured were removed before arrival at the surgical unit in order to check for other life-threatening and bodily wounds. Dale had no indication of his faith except two holy cards of St. Joseph and Guardian Angels and his breathing. I assumed he was Catholic although his dog tags read "no preference."

And so I prayed. I read the St. Joseph card aloud which promised one would not die among enemies. The gunny of Bravo Surgical, a corpsman, and the company commander stood silent. Dale had been flown in, so we were his family. I anointed him, forgave his sins, and told him not to be afraid of the Light - that Jesus would welcome him. Jesus promised, "Today you will be with me in Paradise." The Gospel reading of the following Sunday will forever have new meaning for me.

So often I want to pray to that criminal on the cross beside Jesus: Teach us how to admit our guilt and most importantly, to ask, plead, and cry out, "Jesus, remember me when you come into your Kingdom." "Remember Dale!"

After a couple songs, I said the prayer of Mother Theresa. The fruit of silence is prayer. The fruit of prayer is faith. The fruit of faith is love. The fruit of love is service. The fruit of service is peace. The man before me was no longer a Marine. He was one of the poorest persons in the world because he was about to leave the world behind. We leave this world naked, just as we entered it. We can't even take our body, bones, positions, or our wonderful relationships. How often did Mother Theresa and her sisters simply hold the dying? And that is what we did. It didn't matter what

Dale's faith was or if he even had any faith at all. We beheld a child of God. When I finished the prayer, beloved Dale went silent.

We all just stood there, in awe of the eternal silence. It was such a short moment in time, but one that will be with us forever.

I walked to Mortuary Affairs in another building just a few steps away. Dedicated Marines took out Dale's very few belongings sent with him from the field and placed them on the gurney beside his lifeless body. I saw and held a crucifix that had apparently hung around his neck. The crucifix looked original and was wrapped in Dale's blood. I have never felt so close to the crucifixion of my Lord. As I held that bloody medal, I could only begin to imagine what the Mother of Jesus endured at Jesus' death and still endures today. *And you, yourself, a sword will pierce so that the thoughts and hearts of many may be revealed.* Suddenly, I glanced at the gurney and noticed a Christian medal with five scenes of the life of Jesus and his family. I turned the medal over in my hand and read with stunned heart:

I am Catholic...call a Priest.

I quickly wrote a card for Dale's family and placed it with his personal belongings. I shared the last moments of their beloved Dale's life so they could be there. And they were. And they are. *

Angels directing us.

Angels calling us to be in the light of the World.

Silence and Peace

Bring us Home, Jesus

Bring us Home!

*Dale Burger's mother contacted me fifteen months later. She told me she had received the note tucked in with his body.

Dale Burger Jr. was buried beside his father at Arlington National Cemetery with the Vietnam Veterans. His father died only six months earlier and is buried a few feet away. Both were the recipients of the Purple Heart. (Pictures courtesy of my brother-in-law, Larry Gatlin)

Chapter II

Recalled to Active Duty

My name is Ron Camarda. I am a Catholic Priest, ordained for the Diocese of St. Augustine, Florida. Many people simply call me "Father" or "Padre." I had been serving as the Pastor of St. Patrick's Catholic Church and School for the previous five years. I was also a reserve chaplain for the Personnel Mobilization Team in Jacksonville. I served two months the previous year filling in for a priest chaplain who had been very sick at the Naval Air Station, Jacksonville. Most of my drills were performed at the Naval Hospital in Jacksonville on Fridays and during emergencies.

On July 5, 2004, I received a call from the Reserve Center in New Orleans. They were recalling me to active duty for 365 days or for two years to Iraq. I was stunned. Just two weeks earlier, I had qualified for twenty years of service for retirement purposes. In fact, my paperwork was already in process when I received orders to report for duty on August 2. I thought I was safe. I thought I had fulfilled my duty. I did not want to go to Iraq. So I did what I always have done when my life's course is changing: I complained.

I offered every possible excuse to the Reserve Force Chaplain justifying why I should not go to Iraq. I was not the one to be called for such an assignment. At nearly 45 years of age, I had been passed over for commander, and I was only a reservist. Our diocese had a critical shortage of priests. My parish needed me. My school kids would be devastated. I had more than served my time. I even reasoned that I had season tickets to the Jaguar NFL football games with my Dad.

I also knew if my Bishop removed his endorsement for me to serve in the military, the Navy couldn't compel me to go. Other priests had done this. I did, however, have over 20 years of service. No one had forced me to commit to the Naval Reserves. So I went to my chapel at St. Patrick's, and I sat and listened. "They need you, Ron. You have certain gifts to share with My people." I didn't want to listen, though. I didn't want to hear this. I simply didn't want to go. I asked God to send someone else. God placed it in my heart I was to go to Iraq.

I didn't tell anyone the news until the orders arrived on July 15 that I was to report on August 2. I would be serving with the U.S. Marines in Operation Noble Eagle and Enduring Freedom in Fallujah, Iraq. I could be in Iraq for up to two years, but most likely seven months. I would be attached to Surgical Bravo Company of 1st FSSG, part of a Religious Ministry Team (RMT) that would include a Religious Program Specialist (RP1 Patrick Bowen) and me. Patrick would act as my bodyguard and assist in setting up all religious ministries in the field and camps. Patrick was wonderful. He is the husband of Leanne and the father of three small children, including twin boys who were only five at the time. I managed to delay my departure until the day after my last Mass on August 9. I then flew to California via Norfolk, Virginia. We departed Camp Pendleton on September 2 and arrived in Fallujah, Iraq, four days later.

Fallujah: Padre Camarda and LCDR Michael Warrington, USN, stand in front of the company's first motto, which was changed to "READY TO RECEIVE."

Chapter III

The Beginning of My Black Journal

(Wrestling with God)

My friend, Hazel Yoachim, gave me a black journal. She had often attended my Bible studies at St. Patrick's where I had spent my last five years. Hazel and her husband, Robert, have been married for nearly sixty years.

On the journal's first page, Hazel wrote:

Fr. Ron:

I like this quote-

To thine own self be true, then it must follow as day follows night,

That thou cant's not then be false to any man.

God bless and keep you all, safe –

Hazel Yoachum 7-31-04

Over the next several months, I wrote almost daily in this journal, recording thoughts, offering prayers, and even sketching in the margins. It was the place where I expressed my deepest feelings and raw emotions.

13 August 2004 Norfolk, VA (Naval Station)

How appropriate that I am waiting to start the journey, detached more and more. I will fly to San Diego and prepare at Camp Pendleton before traveling to Iraq.

My mother died four years ago today.
She detached and went to a place I don't know, but I do know.
I love my Mom
Not past tense, but present.

I love you, God.
Last night, we celebrated my friends Patrick and Lourdes' son who died in the womb.
(Patrick and Lourdes were married in Puerto Rico in the mid '90s and I was the celebrant.)

We held him.
We touched him.
We were moved by him.
We named him:
JOHN ISABEL.
Powerful.

Oh give thanks to the Lord, for he is good! For His mercy endures forever.

\- 1 Chronicles 16:34

17 August 2004 **Camp Pendleton**

Preparing to go to Iraq with the Marines

Jesus?!*!

I love you. I am afraid.

I am trying not to be.

From my mother's womb you called me.

This astounds me.

But it is <u>nothing</u> I have done or will do.

It is you who call us all

Out of darkness

Into your glorious light.

Give me strength, O Lord,

and focus to carry out your mission.

Help me to be your face,

your hands

your touch

your eyes

Lead me into your courageous

heart

that was pierced

abused.

O Jesus

You know me,

You probe me,

You create me and you cannot abandon me.

You love me too much to leave me alone.

And yet you love me too much not to leave me alone.

I'm a coward, Lord. I am weak.

You call me, Ron Moses, into the desert.

You lure me. You drive me.

Protect me Lord, from the Evil One.

Lift me up when I am down.

And if I should recoil and sink as I know I will…

SAVE ME!

RESCUE ME!

I love you.

Ron Moses +

For the Lord is good; His mercy is everlasting,

And His truth endures to all generations.

-Psalm 100:5

I read the following quote from the Office of Readings for that 17th day of August:

Every soul of every walk of life and creed receives the just sentence of death and the curse from which Christ our Lord has delivered us. We are all brothers and sisters at war with one another.

Whenever we suffer affliction, we should regard it both as a punishment and as a correction. Our holy Scriptures themselves do not promise us peace, security and rest.

On the contrary, the Gospel makes no secret of the troubles and temptations that await us, but it also says that he who perseveres to the end will be saved.

– Saint Augustine of Hippo

31 August 2004 From Jacksonville to San Diego

(I was granted three days to return to Florida before our departure to Iraq).

Thank you Lord Jesus, for this little respite before the storm. There is joy in the journey. How blessed I am. For I have wonderful family, friends, love, and You, Lord Jesus. Lift me up. Thank you so much for these few days. Gratitude wells up. Bless them, Lord, my closest friends and family. How wonderful You are to me.

Teach me, Jesus, to have courage and to proclaim Your glory, Your promise of love, peace, peace, and more peace. Gently correct me, discipline me and love me. There truly is only one thing I ask of You, O Lord, O Love...to live in your Temple forever, in love, in joy, and in peace. I am not afraid, for You are beside me, above me, within me.

Praise You!   Praise You!   Praise You!
Let the Journey continue. I love YOU!

Ron Moses +

And whatever you ask in My name that I will do, that the Father may be glorified in the Son. –John 14:13

31 August 2004

Prince of Peace Abbey, Oceanside, California

(Outside Camp Pendleton)

Not very still, rather restless
Sitting before You crossed legs, Indian style
Full of Gratitude
You love me, Jesus
Just the way I am
Here and now
Through and through and

You

desire

my love

an insignificant

and imperfect

puny gift

in return.

You are awesome, Lord, Mighty,

Meek, Humble, Gentle,

Loving, Generous, Kind

God.

I do love You, Lord

I do trust You.

I am afraid of suffering

yet my faith grows.

I know you are my source

of food, love, energy, and peace.

Thank You, Lord, for blessings.

Teach me to detach more and more.

Grant me Wisdom.

I love you,

Ron Moses +

1 September 2004

My dorm room on Camp Pendleton

O Jesus,

I am scared.

Help me with this fear.

Show me the way

Help me to prepare

for Your will and Your love in this world.

We have neglected the poor

Have mercy on us

I am nothing

and yet I am Yours

a child

a crying baby.

Lift me up, Lord,

Lift me up!

HM3 Sorrenson with daughter and wife on 2 September 2004

Time to go!

2 September 2004 **March Air Force Base**

Here I sit with a Buddhist dentist, Sook, who is wonderful, on a plane bound for Kuwait and then to IRAQ. The commercial plane is enormous. We boarded single file, weary and sweaty from much packing and waiting. Nine hours and fifty-nine minutes to Frankfurt, Germany. And so the journey continues. It's hard to believe I'm heading into a war zone.

Now on the runway, we go with God's blessing.
I pray, I hope.

My Beloved God,

This was so hard to understand.

I was frightened and extremely weak in faith.

We are flying above the few clouds.

The mountains are elegant on a clear day.

Evening approaches.

Jesus, we are physicians and nurses

and corpsmen and Marines

Touch our hearts and heal our many wounds.

Let us embrace Your

Remarkable Creation

I love You. Your will be done.

To Babylon we travel. Bring us back safe. Alleluia.

Lord, open my lips, that my mouth may proclaim your praise!

- Morning Prayer Praise

3 September 2004

Hurricane Frances Prepares to Ravage Florida

Time is rather odd as we streak through time zones. We look at the world, and we glimpse it like God could. We rush to the future through seven time zones.

We are mostly Marines and the medical battalion, Precious Cargo. This commercial airline carries 278 Marines and sailors to be deployed for six to seven months to Iraq.

Officers and staff naval commissioned officers, NCO, are in either first class or business class. The junior enlisted are literally crammed in the back of the plane. The flight attendants say they are extremely polite and cooperative. This is the most desired assignment for the flight crew. There is no alcohol.

I walk to the back of the plane even though it is difficult to navigate the narrow aisles and cramped conditions. Bless them, Lord. They are only children called to serve our nation that often loses direction. Most of them are 17, 18, 19, or 20 years old. This is an adventure. But are they really ready for the violence and hatred they will face? I gather from my brief encounters with them that some are escaping violence and abuse in their own families. The discipline of the Marine Corps is probably a welcome respite. They really don't have a choice. Many are poor not only in material things; they also suffer deep poverty of spirit.

And this is my mission. **I am to love them equally and abundantly as God chooses.** God really loves them all more than I could ever imagine.

Here I have complained and resisted my calling in conjunction with my name, Ron Moses, to be with them. God is absolutely and incredibly with us. God wants to lavish His children with every good thing, especially a sense of joy.

God truly is good all the time. How can I possibly complain? God only asks me to help release His people from slavery. We all are enslaved by greed, pride, lust, gluttony, anger, envy and bitterness. We both forget and refuse to thank our Creator for our lives.

We are currently flying over Ireland, the birthplace of my grandmother, Mary Josephine Crowley. She was born shortly before the turn of the century and departed as a fourteen-year-old girl to pursue love, God, food, and freedom. She married my grandfather, Moses Duffy, out of love and choice. She adored her husband. At the age of 58, he died suddenly. I have never known him. Or have I? My confirmation name is Moses. Patrick is the Moses of Ireland. Moses' brother was Aa**ron**. I am Ron Moses +.

You, O Lord, work marvels in me, through me, despite me. You are magnificent, Oh God. You made me; You knew me. You kept me alive, long before I came to be. You welcome me home. You cherish me. You embrace me and kiss me.

You only ask that I be a conduit of your love to all I meet and all you place in my path. As we pass over the Isle of Man and the Irish Sea, I rejoice. You truly love us, God. You have not abandoned us. You call us into being. Wow!

I am your instrument of peace.

For I, the Lord your God,
will hold your right hand, saying to you,
"Fear not, I will help you."
– Isaiah 41:13

A stop in Frankfurt, Germany

Christopher, a young Private First Class turned 20 years old today. I gave him my St. Christopher medal which was presented to me by the women of St. Patrick's. The Navy Emblem was on the back of the medal. Christopher was thrilled. Therefore, I am thrilled.

4 September 2004 **Saturday in Kuwait**

Oh my, it is hot!

5 September 2004 **Al Taqaadam, Iraq**

This has been rough.

Chapter IV

September in Fallujah

(Purging of my soul)

6 September 2004

I am in Al Taqaadam, Iraq (known as TQ).

When we arrived on a C-130, the helicopters were flailing, the Marines were screaming at us, and the power was out. It was hot. We initially anticipated boarding some helicopters; we were placed in a barren dirt space, and then … we weren't expected.

Now we await transport to Fallujah. This won't be easy. We number about 52 sailors and Marines, and we travel by convoy tonight. The journey will take three to four hours even though it is just eighteen miles.

It only takes a few to make life miserable for the majority. It has been difficult for me to write, largely because the climate is so darn uncomfortable. Within an hour, I go from feeling extremely cold to being so hot, sticky, and dusty. This is a very arid area. The heat is oppressive. How did people manage before air conditioning?

I don't want to complain, so I won't. However, some common difficulties include intense heat, portable toilets, cold tents at night, and food that is not easily digested.

It amazes me how much food is wasted. I am so hungry before tasting the food, but after a few bites, I lose my appetite.

So often on this trip, we are unaware of what is to come.

I'm a bit older than many: I'm trying not to complain, just noting. This is really an adventure.

God is with us. There is nothing to fear.

We finally received a tent. It was Saturday night, and I needed to celebrate the Sunday Mass.

We celebrated Mass in a dark, unoccupied tent.

It was difficult to bring about the Word of God. I didn't feel particularly wise, although the Sacred Scripture spoke of wisdom. When I opened the wine, it exploded! Glory to God in the highest! Peace to his people on earth! What else could go wrong? I begged God not to answer that question until after it happened.

We lifted up the people of the Bahamas devastated by Frances the Hurricane. Please, God, protect my family in Florida.

I love you, Jesus.

Guide my hand to write from your Heart and my heart.

Ron Moses +

My grace is sufficient for you, for My strength is made perfect in weakness.

- 2 Corinthians 12:8

On the evening of September 6, we took a convoy to Camp Fallujah. The sweat, fear, terror, dirt, dust, prayer, sleepiness, watchfulness, cramped conditions, and organized chaos suffocated my ability to write clearly about it at the time. It was as much a journey within my being as it was traveling on the terrifying and dusty road in Iraq.

It was dark, but I could see the other men and women around me, breathing the same dusty and stale air, crammed on the exposed five-ton truck. We were not very well protected. Was I seeing the flickering lights of their souls? If our enemies had known we were doctors and nurses and the like, they could have inflicted a catastrophic blow to their enemy, the United States of America. I was the only one unarmed. Patrick was close by as my only physical defense. I reached for the wooden carved cross in my pocket. The cross was my only comfort.

Fifty of us (the first half of our company) were so relieved to leave Al Taqaadam, a secluded camp in Iraq. We just wanted to get on with the journey which would take us to our 'home' for the next seven months. However, as we gathered in the twilight hours, we sat through the unnerving convoy brief. If we hadn't realized how dangerous the endeavor was before this moment, we were quickly convinced after the brief. The Colonel met us with his confident convoy crew. The crew, made up of young Marines and a corpsman, were already hardened by desert, dust and war. Some, however, were obviously going on their first convoy.

During the brief, we were so alarmed that we anxiously followed every command. We checked and rechecked our gas masks. Others rehearsed in their minds how to use their firearms. We reviewed our training and all of the reactions we would have to undertake if we came under attack. We had repeatedly practiced this at Camp Pendleton less than a week before, yet now we were here in the flesh and blood. Many others had suffered amputations and even died from attacks on convoys.

One of the Officers in Charge discovered there was a Catholic Priest with Bravo Surgical Company. I received word to say a prayer before our departure. As I stood next to a portable toilet, I felt the urgent need to urinate. I was extremely nervous about the impending departure of our convoy. All of us lined up with the enlisted in the first three rows and the officers in the back two. As sweat beaded off my brow and trickled down my back, I began to think about what I should pray. I was tired of the whole thing, and we hadn't even arrived yet. Then the convoy commander gathered all of us together and gave assurance that none of us would perish, as only a Marine could inflict such confidence. It really was a pretty day. The sun was just setting, and the heat was not too extreme. Maybe my internal prayer was cooling us. Then I was called to pray to the group.

Beloved, believe me when I tell you I am not conventional. God never allows me such peace. I pray with my whole creative spirit and soul. I give it my all. I have been accused and mocked so often for my style. In a peculiar way, I don't blame people. If I were not me, I wonder if I would be taken aback by my different and unique style. However, I was living each day as if it could be my first, only, and last day. I wanted the prayer to come from God. I looked at all of the Marines and sailors before me with heads bowed. Most of them were Christian, with some Muslims, Jews, Atheists, and at least one Buddhist dentist. How was I to pray for such a group of people? What had they in common? They were all born, and they would all most certainly die. They were all citizens of our beloved nation. So, I gave a generic prayer. I sang Taps and remembered those who put their lives on the line that day, especially our convoy guides in whom our trust was placed.

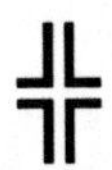

Thanks and Praise

For our Days
'Neath the Sun
'Neath the Stars
'Neath the Sky
As we Go
This we Know
God is Nigh!

Then I sang the third verse of the Star Spangled Banner and proclaimed an "Amen," to which the troops were quiet for two to three seconds and then shouted out together, "AMEN!"

O thus be it ever, when free men shall stand,
Between their loved homes and the war's desolation;
Blessed with vict'ry and peace,
may the heaven's rescued land
Praise the Power that has made
and preserved us a nation.
Then conquer we must, if our cause it is just,
And this be our motto:
IN GOD IS OUR TRUST,
And the Star - Spangled Banner
In triumph shall wave
O'er the land of the free and the home of the brave.

And so we traveled all night on that convoy. Hearts pounded, and we felt as if we were being stalked. It was a very dark night. In the months to come, I would take many convoys at night and some in daylight. Each one was always a cause for concern. It was a new kind of prayer for me. It was like the water I used to hydrate me. Every breath and every glance were prayers of great dimension and intensity. Even praying the Rosary took on new significance and need. It is hard to explain total peace and yet total fear without returning to Psalm 131:

Truly I have set my soul in silence and peace.

As an infant rests in its mother's arms

Even so my soul

O Israel (those who wrestle with God), hope in the Lord now and forever!

So often I imagined myself sitting in the arms of God as a toddler. God, whom I call "Father," would see me through. In God I trust. In God I trust. In God I trust!

8 September 2004 **Birth of Mary**

O Jesus,

I am filled with zeal and anger.

I don't trust our leaders.

They are just like me.

We are in Camp Fallujah. Bravo Surgical's field hospital is a narrow, hard (or cement) building. Our quarters are across the dirt road. The commanding officer, LCDR Michael Warrington (Medical Supply Corps), and the Gunnery Sergeant constantly supervise improvements to the physical "campus" in order to provide the most efficient and life-saving hospital possible. We have two operating rooms and five major trauma stations with the capacity to increase to ten. The hospital includes a dental room, a combat stress room, an x-ray room, a supply building, two wards, command and radio rooms, and a meeting room often used for overflow.

Outside are various trucks and ambulances. The hospital is designed to have the wounded brought through the front doors. Before they enter Bravo Surgical, their weapons must be removed. At the height of the battle, we used over 50 beds including an overflow building. Mortuary Affairs was among our buildings, although it was considered to be a separate unit.

After the Battle for Fallujah, the overflow ward was converted to a club that served non-alcoholic beverages. Our unit surroundings reminded me of the television show "M.A.S.H." without distiller.

9 September 2004

I met Father Bill Devine yesterday evening. He is a wonderful and devoted priest. His eyes are filled with compassion. He has been in Iraq seven months and has served both the grunts and the Al Fallujah Base Camp. He came every second or third week to celebrate Sunday Mass on Tuesday and Wednesday. Bill is weathered yet saintly looking. I hope to gain great insight into his depth of ministry so I can serve without complaining.

I need to relax and breathe in God's love.

Evening

In some ways, I'm enjoying myself. If I look ahead to returning, I feel overwhelmed. It is extremely hot here, but there is air conditioning. I can't imagine how people survived before A/C! Yes, it is noisy, but we adjust like we did aboard ship.

Iraq,
The trip, journey of Abraham
Babylonian Captivity
I love you, God. Show me the way.

10 September 2004

Early this morning, one of our nurses, Sarah Yuengling, heard news of her father's death. She had expected it, but no one is ever truly prepared for the death of a parent. The trip into the heart of Iraq was exhausting and dangerous. It would be such a lonely and distressing trip back alone. I am not sure I would even consider it if my own father had died.

Sarah decided to stay. I hope I would make the same choice. There could not have been a battle buddy for her like our original journey here, someone to share in the experience of traveling to the unknown. It would be emotional. It would be a long journey, and there was no funeral planned. Isn't it so often the case that family dynamics get tangled up in the immediate aftermath of death?

If we have faith, we come to understand that death is a kind of birth. Many deployed sailors and Marines will greet their children for the first time when they arrive home after six to fifteen months in the desert.

Life will be different when Sarah returns home in about seven months. Her father will no longer be living among the rest of us who will eventually die ourselves. I remember that my whole perspective on life changed after my mother died in 2000. When I put on vestments made with her own seamstress gifts, I pause at that moment and reflect on my mother's life. The celebration is affected by this pause.

When someone is born, the family is forever changed. The family takes a new course as it makes room for the new life. Death works the same way. When a breathing life leaves this world, the world must then adjust to the absence of the person.

As the scripture says, we are all part of the world like a body. If the toe hurts, the rest of the body hurts. If the eyesight is lost, the whole body can be in darkness. If the hearing goes, the whole body is in silent isolation and imminent danger. And so the death of a loved one is a dangerous condition for our families, our nation, and the world.

Out here in the desert of Iraq, I physically minister to the wounded and dying. Some wounds are hidden, like the wound of grief, anger, separation, and loss of peace to war.

John, father of Sarah

died last night in Florida.

Sarah is here in Fallujah, Iraq

Grief in a desert

Detached from family support

Yet we are a new family

quite attuned to death and danger.

O God, teach us to reach out to your love

Comfort us in our temporary state of despair and grief

Envelope us with your love

Touch our souls in this pain that we may rejoice in life

that you gift us with.

Thank you O Beloved for John Yuengling

and his seven children and their families.

"I will never forget you my people,

I have carved you in the palm of my hand."

Isaiah the Prophet

And later that day I wrote:

Love in Iraq

Alone

To ponder life

Lost

Waiting to be found

Waiting to be found

Strong is love

Strong is love

Stronger than hate

Stronger than despair

Stronger than poverty

They all drain our lives

Love

Leave it all on the table

Let it die

And God will lift it up, forever and ever.

God is good! All the time!

14 September 2004

May I boast of nothing but the cross on which Jesus, my beloved friend and creator, was hung. And yet I still complain bitterly about my lot. Here I am in the desert where simple bodily functions like expulsion and washing can be so laborious and unpleasant.

In minutes, I can forget the joy of encountering Our Lord in the desert. I am so fickle, so spineless. O Beloved Jesus, what is it that you see in me, in those around me?

I trip on my tongue thousands of times in a day. Mortars fly all around me as we try to fight the enemy who seems invisible. Back and forth, back and forth they fly. The saying, "an eye for an eye, a tooth for a tooth," seems to permeate this theater. Good Christians seem intent, like King David, on destroying the enemy, the Philistines.

Yet, in the midst of the atrocities of a just war, King David turns away and commits that mortal sin of adultery and conspiracy and murder. Will we ever learn to live in peace? Is it possible for Muslims, Jews, Christians, and Buddhists to ever live in peace? Many cry out to you, O Lord. They believe you are deaf to their cries. They do not understand. We shepherds have failed to tell them.

How can I do this, Lord? Nothing seems easy. Within me, I have the source of the Fountain that you bore in me. Yet, I feel like a dried-up piece of fruit…useless.

O God, give me the Wisdom to pronounce your Word. Give me the ability to speak 'peace' in the midst of anger and hostility.

You, O Lord, are the True Prince of Peace. Make me your instrument of peace. More violence and outrage is brewing, but you ALONE, O Lord will bring about peace in Your time, Your way, and Your love.

Bless us, O Lord.
Let us not be far from you.
Give me courage.
Deepen the Love within me,
a Love that was purchased at great cost. Amen

I love you,

Ron Moses +

+ Kevin Shea

Major Kevin Shea died this evening on his birthday. He received Eucharist on Saturday evening. I was only thirty yards away from the impact of the incoming rocket. I walked with his body and blood.

My Redeemer has a claim upon my love, and I do not forget how he questioned Peter, and asked: Do you love me Peter? Then feed my sheep. He asked this once, then again and then a third time. He inquired about his love, and then he gave him work to do; for the greater one's love is, the easier is the work.

– St. Augustine

16 September 2004

+ Andy Stern, 1st LT *

+ Cpl Rimaki

**When a name appears with a cross before it, this respectfully indicates the person has died. This is how I recorded names in a small green journal carried in my cargo pockets along with my wooden cross. Sometimes, I later wrote in more detail in my black journal.*

17 September 2004

How can I possibly write of the wrongs I witnessed today? First, we waited forever for four to eight inbound casualties. Frankly, we expected the worst, but after encountering men who had a "military fender-bender," we were almost disappointed. How could this be? The last five days have been one tragedy after another. Faces are shot off, and IEDs (improvised explosive devices) decapitate, bludgeon, and disfigure. These roadside bombs are rigged with shrapnel like screws and twisted metal… constructed by twisted minds. The insurgents say they do it all in the name of God... horrific, diabolical. Then, there are the *'inborn rocket mortars'* with absolutely no precision, thousands launched monthly into our base which is less than a mile square.

One explosion missed twenty sleeping Marines and sailors by a few feet right before my eyes. I had just emerged from the bathroom trailers. The sight of another explosion shocked me so completely that I cried out, "Is there a Chaplain here?" A female religious program specialist who had arrived two days earlier reminded me, "Padre, You ARE the chaplain!"

Today a rocket hit about thirty yards away, shortly after Mass while I was hearing confessions. One of my flock died, and another was seriously hurt. After the destructive blast, I was very close to it, with smoke and fire still rising in the air. I ran toward the impact of the explosion. I was confused, unsure of my role or myself.

I walked and ran with the first casualty, barely tracing the cross on his body. He will be fine, I reassured myself. The second Marine's face was covered; he was physically dead. I ran alongside as the stretcher oozed blood, drop by drop. Just three days before, Kevin received the Body and Blood of Jesus at Mass. And so those drops on the sidewalk were drops of Jesus' blood, but I didn't know it at the time.

I ran the hundred yards to the Bravo Surgical field hospital. The religious program specialist ran beside me with tears streaming down her cheeks. It felt so odd to be ministering as we were running. I was not just running physically; I was also running from sheer terror. I was running from my confusion and outright fear and responsibilities. We were in a war, and I was no longer afraid. Yet, I cringed at the thought of my own body experiencing the devastating blows of mental and physical pain of injuries or death caused by hatred.

Later that night, I saw the blood stains on the sidewalk from the explosion. Yet, by the next morning, the stains had disappeared, blended with dirt, maybe washed, yet stained into my soul forever.

I need that blood for myself, that blood of Kevin Michael Shea, a Marine, a husband, a father, a son, a brother. Kevin broke bread with us on Saturday evening. He was thrilled to partake of the Body and Blood . . . that now returns to the dust just as Jesus' Blood absorbed in the dirt during the Crucifixion.

And then today, shortly after reviewing possible scenarios in a mass casualty drill, they came. Nothing prepares us for the gruesome details that mark our souls and spirits forever. Injured and dead they came - blown up. One man had a leg amputated whose life was still in danger. Our emotions of humor shocked us as we desperately struggled to grasp our reality. We had never experienced anything like this. One man had a shrapnel injury to his neck. Ah Jesus! You give these doctors, nurses, corpsmen and

Marines the ability to heal through tedious, but effective medical crisis interventions.

And then there is me,
a chaplain
a little priest,
struggling to be more selfless,
less selfish,
and more saintly.

Jesus, what can I say? What can I do when I am delivered two men, one Iraqi Muslim translator and a young Baptist Marine slopped into a truck, intertwined and dead? What prayers can I possibly offer? I anointed with Christian prayer the 20-year-old young man whose twin brother was somewhere out here in Iraq. I said Muslim prayers for the translator, "Allah be praised! Allah be praised! Allah be praised!" However, the most meaningful prayer for me had no words. I looked into the eyes of those around me, both officers and enlisted and those who had to move the gruesome, yet holy, remains of these persons to the bags and then to the morgue. My eyes were moist, and intense feelings gripped and stung me.

When, O Lord, will you deliver us from such evil?
When, O Lord, will you tolerate such hatred no more?

It seems it will never end and yet we must evoke hope, peace and forgiveness. Even the word, forgiveness, weighs us down. Anger and bitterness swirl like tornadoes, plowing down all in their path. Yet the sun still rises, and the moon is so ominous. Hurricanes devastate my state.

Give us courage, Lord, to stop this deceitful power just as you stopped it on the cross.

This is all too brutal. Our Bravo Surgical team includes Jews, Christians, Agnostics, and at least one Buddhist and a Muslim. All nationalities unite and work together to heal. Can't we defend ourselves from such misguided enemies with just love? Where does this deep-seated bitterness, lack of love and craziness originate?

Only you, Lord Jesus, can save us, ***only you.***

Goodnight, my Beloved.

Protect me with your love.

Please be in my dreams.

Let me be your servant.

Give me Wisdom to be

your Love in Hell. Give me courage.

I love you,

Ron Moses +

ر **Sammy** *(Muslim, Interpreter)*

\+ **Cpl Christopher Ebert** *(Brother Tim in Iraq)*

HN1 Joseph Worley *(Christ prayer)*

Richard Sullivan, LCPL – *Catholic*

+Christopher Ebert

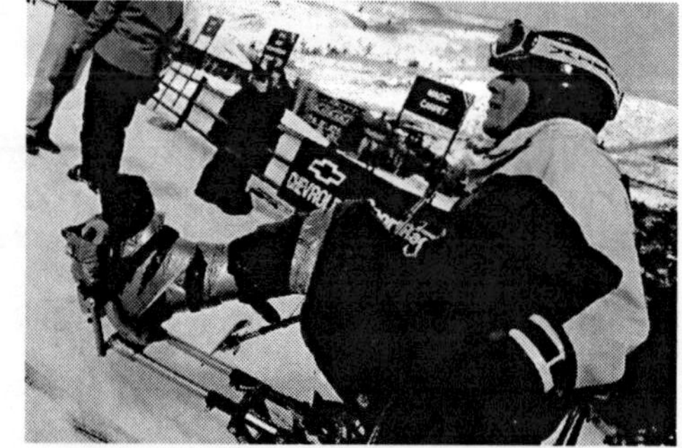

I mistakenly thought Joseph Worley died, but am most happy to report this picture was taken March 2006. Thanks be to God!

20 September 2004 — Camp Fallujah, Iraq

Do I really love you, Jesus? You know I do, but do I have the wisdom and courage to comprehend this reality?

Here I am

Far from home

Hospital in the field

Casualties of war

Loss of blood

Fight absorbed into the dust

Anger and bitterness still here?

Peaceful for a moment

Mortars shooting

Bombs exploding

Still calm

Until they are brought in

one or two KIA

one or two maimed and bloody

one or two fragments or scratch

all wounded emotionally, psychologically, physically, and spiritually,

This, this is not a popular war

Hardly a warm fuzzy

In camp we never touch

The child

The lifestyle

The soul

Controlled environment secured like an island

Deep in the isolation

Lost

Sure we have communication

Yet all are monitored

We are not free

To tell it how it is (and that may be a good thing)

Ah Jesus,

What shall we do?

What shall we do?

These people in general are wired to fight

Losing sight of the original cause

But then again, have we forgotten?

As long as we go back to 9/11

As justification for

thousands dead and tens of thousands wounded

we need to forgive…and move on

No one can win through revenge

money

or an eye for an eye.

Help us we pray,

to see through eyes

compassionate

observant

compliant to You O God.

Let us love one another

Let us pray for one another. Amen

23 September 2004 (Same day, Thursday)

A week has passed since a rocket crashed into a Marine. I fed him the Bread of Life and the Blood of Christ. I anointed Kevin after his death and saw his spirit ascend to heaven. I am quite confident that Jesus takes him, loves him, and breathes life into him.

Whoever dies and believes in me will live.
And whoever lives and believes in me will never die.
- Jesus

Strange, but I don't fully believe that Kevin died. He simply walked through the door. He already experiences Ami, his beloved wife, and Michael and Brenna, his children in heaven.
O God, you are so good to us, so good.
God is near to our cry, our grief, and our war upon one another.
God is near to our despair.
God is near to those who love him.
Rest in Love
Rest in Love
BE NOT AFRAID!

24 September 2004 **Friday – Yom Kippur**

God our Father

You conquer the darkness of ignorance

by the light of your Word.

Strengthen within our hearts the faith you have given us;

Let not temptation ever quench the fire

that your love has enkindled within us.

We ask this through our Lord Jesus Christ,

Your Son, who lives and reigns

with you and the Holy Spirit

one God, forever and ever. Amen

-Prayer from the Liturgy of the Hours

I wrote the following letter to the People of my Diocese:

Beloved of St. Augustine Diocese,

Here I am!

A statement. A question. An exclamation.

I am attached to Bravo Surgical Company, which is a hospital in the center of Iraq in the town of Al Fallujah, filled with hatred, insurrectionists, people and Marines. Here at Bravo Surgical, about 100 of us are available for the Marines, sailors, and civilians who encounter car bombs, rockets, gunfire and whatever evil devices are created to rip apart the body. Many of the bombs, including suicide bombers, are filled with deadly shrapnel that can mangle legs, arms, feet, hands and internal organs. It is amazing to me how the corpsmen, surgeons, doctors and nurses sustain the lives of many of them and start the healing process before medically evacuating them to other hospitals on their way to their homes in the U.S. The evil ones go to detention centers, but where the civilian foreigners go, it is hard to determine.

I never knew how much blood there was in the face. This Bravo Surgical Team is neither for the faint of heart nor those queasy about blood.

The operating rooms are quite sterile, but then when two to six or more are brought in and some go to surgery, blood drips on the floor, stretchers, the gloves of the good medical staff, and the patients themselves. Like a horror movie, pools of blood ooze under the door for a few moments, before being miraculously cleaned up. Here, everyone pitches in. The surgeons often swab the decks, and the nurses comfort with great compassion, healing not only with their skills, but with genuine love and pastoral care beyond them.

Sometimes we even treat our enemies with the same care. This week we treated two people who less than an hour before, tried to plant a horrendous bomb that was intended to kill and maim our own troops in the most evil and gruesome way. My emotions are so varied including tremendous anger and disgust, and I am the chaplain! I must choose to manage my emotions. I must love my enemies. And so as a chaplain I look into the eyes of my shipmates with intensity, thanking them without words and encouraging them with hope that love and good will prevail.

How did Jesus forgive them as they harshly nailed his hands? Blood is red when released from the body; it is the color of super heated fire and evokes unleashed anger. How does His mother forgive as the blood splatters and drips upon her? She is like our surgeons going deep, massaging the heart and keeping the service *member alive until God says it is done. To die before he reaches the bloody cross of a pulpit would allow the infectious hatred and evil to spread.*

And so, the cross is truly the resting place - so dark, so alone and so desolate. And yet He whispers through the excruciating pain, "Father, forgive them, they don't know what they do." We must say of our enemies, "Forgive them, Lord God, they don't know what they do."

And then there are times when the Marines drive up with lifeless, breathless bodies that once held life, breath and blood.

In this dusty, dry terrain, blood, sweat and saliva blend quickly into the land, the ground. They are absorbed forever. Oh sure, we return the bodies as best we can to the families, but the blood remains, embedded in the land and in our hearts and painfully, in our fragile minds.

The choice is simple, and yet impossible: bitterness or hope. Allah is not praised in bitterness or in revenge. Allah is praised with forgiveness. God is love. And love will absorb all.

The Marines use the term "Fallen Angel" to indicate a Marine, sailor or soldier who dies, falls to the ground.

In the psalms we sing, "The Lord upholds all who fall, and raises up all who are bowed down." – *Psalm 145:14*

I have anointed with the holy oils too many with names like Kevin, Christopher, Sammy, and Andy who were called 'fallen angels.' Yet, weren't we created to be more than angels? God raises us up. God creates us in the Divine Image.

Many others are anointed. Last weekend at the Holy Eucharist, I anointed those returning home this week. They have seen so much death and destruction these past seven months that they needed the healing of Jesus. Emotional scars and bleeding sores can cause great physical sickness and deterioration. Faith can heal. Just ask Jesus.

Seeing the vulnerability of the human body and the resilience, I recognize my own internal sin and weaknesses. I find myself more tolerant of the annoying habits of others, and Marines have a number of them.

There are moments I wish to cling to, but if I do I could not survive. The wounded come in like our breath and I release them like our breath.

So often I am captivated for a fleeting moment when I look into the eyes of the Marine, sailor or soldier: moist, intense, confused, enraged, compassionate, angry, disgusted, or unforgiving. I am touched to my core. I am beginning to understand how God must love us, especially in our imperfections and our resistance to the glory of love. If our own infant had these same intense feelings and emotions, we wouldn't care. We would simply love the child. Yet when we get older, we want to judge those feelings and emotions, which are simply the same. They only belong to a bigger child. Love will cleanse and heal.

Jesus is here.

Where else could I be?

Who else could I be?

When is now.

My love for you all in the Diocese of St. Augustine is so intense and full of gratitude. Your prayers are being put to incredible use. God will repay you with more. Be generous with your love.

Peace, Joy, Love,

Father Ron Camarda +

P.S. On Eagle's Wings and Be Not Afraid are songs we all love to sing out here! We especially like the part about 'walking through the desert and the flames.'

27 September 2004 **Monday – Camp Fallujah**

We are not free
To walk without fear
It kind of irritates me
I am one of the only troops
Without an M-16 or a pistol
No serial number
No magazine
No bullets
Does faith count?
It suits me
But my RP (bodyguard) will have none of that
And that could be good
After all, a defense is required
Otherwise there is no God Doc!
As we were returning the short mile
from the FOB (forwarding operating base)
as they call it
I was in the back of an open truck
used to haul anything from chow
to supplies and troops
Today it carried me.
I prefer more armor, but it was nice to see
Until a vehicle from the other direction didn't understand
that these seven military vehicles were waving them off

Then there was shouting and the rifles already cocked and ready and aimed
I hit the deck looking through the front window
My heart racing
And the car that almost wasn't
Passed close
Overloaded with Iraqi civilians
Laughing and joking freely as if there was no problem
Not aware that their lives were almost terminated

O the problems and the fog of war

You see, we are not free
We are in a danger zone
We are afraid
Enclosed in walls and behind guns
Surrounded by enemies and IED's
Every once in awhile,
a rocket or mortar slips in that hits a random target
Or lonely imprisoned heart
And we mourn and move on
To our living in our open air prison where
We are not free
To walk without fear
It kind of irritates me
for explosions are near.

28 September 2004

What am I doing here?

I know, but I still resist.

29 September 2004 **Saints Michael, Gabriel & Rafael**

I attended a Warrior Transition Brief for those who will be returning to "normal" life after being in a combat zone for over six months. The chaplains present this seminar at the end of the tour. It can only be done a few weeks before the servicemen actually leave the combat zone. In a few months, I will give this brief to my command and to others. Some of the questions raised are: "What impact will the stress of being dangerously close to death every day for months have on us? How will we adjust to not having a firearm everywhere including the showers, the chow hall and the chapel? It is hard enough to be separated from loved ones and children for such a long period. What will the impact be?"

The nightmare of war will likely continue when we return home. Alcohol consumption is not allowed in Iraq (and yet it is still smuggled in). We might see an onslaught of alcohol-related problems upon our return. There are many roadblocks to a healthy transition back to "normal" life. These issues include but are by no means conclusive:

- Alcohol abuse
- Fantasies
- Criticisms
- Unresolved issues
- Expectations
- Failure to avoid the "Who had it worse" game with others
- Lack of driving a car for seven months
- Infidelity

This war is different than previous wars because we are encouraged to share our stories. Despite all of the negatives of this war, some positive aspects of it include:

- Focus on the military mission
- Unit cohesion and lasting friendships
- Delivery of food, aid, and medicine to an oppressed people
- Close contact with family via e-mails, care packages, and phone calls
- Patriotic feelings
- Maturation

I will greatly ponder how to approach this upcoming brief.

The moon, the sun in Mesopotamia
Looks different here
The dust in the air is thick
A fog of sand or dirt
The cloud seems to permeate even our minds
Depression
Wrestling with thoughts and moods
Wrestling with God? Denial?
I left about a month ago
And yet I really left two months ago
A journey
Just like Abraham traveled
Only I have no children
And I will have no grandchildren
To tell my stories to
Yet many call me "Father Ron"
Many know me and greet me
This man is weak and feeble of mind
And yet I am able to touch others and redirect
Instrument of God's peace I am used.

Life is not glamorous here. We use plastic plates and eat with plastic utensils. When we shower or use the "head" (jargon for bathroom), it isn't pleasant. Sometimes, after walking into the bathroom, I leave immediately because the foul stench is so overpowering. I often dread getting out of my rack in the morning because I don't want to face the extreme heat or cold, lines or dirty heads with racing stripes. Marines in the field can be a little gross. Ordinary daily trials include enduring various bodily and field odors and keeping athlete's feet in check. Another great challenge is experiencing intense waves of homesickness, especially the painful feelings of missing my loved ones.

I am mellowing with each passing day. Hopefully, the image of Christ in me is becoming more apparent. Truly, I am no saint, but I do feel much more patient as time goes on. Patience is essential in Iraq, because there are lines for food, lines for the exchange, lines for the laundry, lines for working out, lines for transportation, lines for a shower, lines for the telephone and e-mail, and lines for the post office, to name a few.

Chapter V

"Acta non Verba"

(Steady as she goes!)

I have been in Iraq for 24 days. I contemplate the journey of my life, the past that has led to this present dry and terror-ridden place.

In July of 1977, I arrived at the U.S. Merchant Marine Academy as a plebe candidate. The Academy was abuzz with reporters most of that year because the first women were to graduate from any federal service academy. I was just thrilled to be there, but I was definitely scared. I had never even been on a ship before. I was asked if I preferred the engine side of a ship or the deck side. I chose deck because I knew I wasn't good with my hands. My first required courses would be engineering. I was in big trouble.

At the very first Academy gathering, we all dressed in black shoes, black socks, khaki shorts, and baseball caps. The entire class then heard, "Look to your right. Look to your left. One of you won't graduate!" I gasped inside. I had survived indoctrination and Acceptance Day. My father had been unable to make it to the Academy until a couple of weeks after the big day when we put on the Merchant Marine Insignia. He was shocked that I was down to less than 135 pounds in my uniform, but I could sense his great pride in me. At times, however, I wondered if I was going to make it. I didn't share with my father that I was failing most of my classes.

I had struggled with a learning disability from childhood. My reading skills were atrocious due to an infection I had suffered as an infant. My hand-eye coordination was very poor. I had always dreaded sports with baseballs and footballs. Whenever I attempted to catch a ball, it usually smashed into my face.

My reading comprehension skills were also very deficient. The courses that required rope handling, wire splicing and ship handling severely taxed my limited coordination. Other classmates had begun to drop out of school. I dreaded the consequences of personal failure. This opportunity would come around only once in my lifetime. I deeply yearned for success. Under the circumstances, I took refuge in prayer and solitude.

In every spare moment, I retreated to the Mariners Chapel and sat in the downstairs Catholic room. It was only yards away from the Long Island Sound. I visited the chapel during my free class period each day to sit and think. I was almost always alone. This peaceful time became an essential part of my life and was soon a non-negotiable priority of my time, regardless of my busy schedule or time constraints. Sometimes, I was behind in schoolwork, but my daily hour in the chapel always felt like time well spent. These times of prayer, along with Eucharist, were the nourishment my soul both longed for and needed in order to survive every week at the Academy.

During my junior and senior years at the Academy, I sailed on four Merchant ships during two six-month deployments. I had the opportunity to visit ports in Africa, Europe, Mexico and Israel. Only two midshipmen sailed on these commercial ships at a time. I worked on the deck side learning how to navigate and observe cargo operations for my licensure as a Third Mate of oceangoing vessels with unlimited tonnage.

While at sea, I often explored the ports I visited. Most of my two sea years were spent on the East, West and South coasts of Africa, combined with a few months in Europe. On two occasions, something happened that would set my life's course to bring me where I am today. On April 8, 1979, I was on a ship on the East Coast of Africa near Tanzania. I had just finished reading the Bible that I had started during the seventh grade. I really did have a reading problem! After closing my Bible, I stepped out onto the fantail of the SS Christopher Lykes. It was a relatively calm night in port, and I savored a moment of quiet reflection, as I had recently been exposed to extreme poverty during this deployment. All of a sudden, I became aware of the most glorious and bountifully beautiful full moon. As I followed the moon's reflection, it seemed to pierce my being. The feeling was one of both extreme joy and sorrow simultaneously, with every other imaginable emotion mingled in as well. I felt enveloped with love, but I was also very frightened and terrified. And yet, I was at peace. I didn't share this experience with anyone at the time, as I was unsure of its meaning to my life.

I returned to school at the Academy for six months. Afterwards, I was sent on my second sixth-month internship deployment. My ship, the USS Del Rio, had been in port on the west coast of Africa and was moored to the docks in Monrovia, Liberia. Late one night, I finished reading the book, The Sword and the Scalpel, an impressive story about a chaplain from the Korean War. I ventured out onto the fantail for a breath of fresh air as I had done numerous times before. I was completely unaware of the date. As I stood alone in the dark night, I glanced upward and saw the full moon's stunning reflection on the water. I immediately attempted to look away from this sight, but it was too late. The effect of seeing the moon's reflection on the water ripped through me in exactly the same terrifying way as it had the previous time. I literally crawled back to my cabin and opened my small journal to record the experience. To my utter shock and disbelief, the date was the exact day of my identical experience on a ship just one year earlier. My journal entry from that day had been, "I spoke to my Lord today." I was speechless. I then wrote, "Whatever you want, Lord."

As before, I didn't share my experience with anyone. My deep thirst for Sacred Scriptures became insatiable. I continued to court my girlfriend, Karen, and intended to marry her the year after graduation. The problem with my plan, however, was that it was not God's plan. My charted course through life would eventually veer in a much different direction.

The U.S. Merchant Marine Academy has a motto: ***"Acta non Verba"*** which translates to "Deeds not Words." The motto is very similar to the cliché: *Actions speak louder than words.*

Graduation was fast approaching, and I began to make decisions about my future. Rather than waiting in Union Halls for a ship after graduation, I applied to the Maritime Graduate Program with the U.S. Coast Guard. My dad had been sick, and I was financially strapped. Also, my fiancée did not want me to sail. When I was guaranteed a Marine Safety Office in Jacksonville, Florida, I made the commitment. During the graduation ceremony, with my family present, all of my classmates (except one other and myself) took the U.S. Navy oath. My friends encouraged me to stand, but I knew it wouldn't be right. The Vice Admiral for the Coast Guard had flown to the ceremony to swear the two of us in, but we were initially overlooked. However, someone noted the "slip up" (probably the Vice Admiral). He walked to the podium and said, "So where are they?" The two of us quickly stood. There was a slight pause, and then the Admiral responded, "See how selective we are in the Coast Guard?" That was June 22, 1981. By 2004, I had remained in the Naval and Coast Guard Reserves on and off active duty for 27 years, going all the way back to Acceptance Day, 1977.

In December of 1982, the Coast Guard in Jacksonville sent me to South Korea to inspect oil rigs under construction for the U.S. Merchant Marine fleet. Because of my experience with stability tests and the Maritime Academy, I was the most qualified in our office. Talk about being afraid. I was terrified!

After managing to survive that three month experience, I happily visited Hawaii on my way home. My new fiancée, Linda, flew out to meet me. She had been a high school friend and had graduated from the Air Force Academy in 1981. In Hawaii, I had a reunion with Father John Newton (Navy Chaplain at the Academy) who was stationed there at the time. I am not exactly sure what happened to my heart during that visit. After returning home, however, I knew my ship was headed in the wrong direction.

A few months later, I shared with Linda my need to try the seminary. Even though she was Methodist, she understood I needed to make the effort. She continues to be a very close friend to this day. One day after confiding in Linda my desire to enter the priesthood, I attended Mass at Christ the King Catholic Church in Jacksonville. I was confused, and I didn't know where to turn or what to do. And then, as I had learned to do at the Mariners Chapel, I sunk into deep reflection and prayer. I was startled to see a priest standing over me when I opened my eyes. He simply asked if I was contemplating becoming a priest. I was shocked. I calmly told him I was considering the possibility but I felt unsure of myself. He persuaded me to attend an upcoming three-day Cursillo retreat.

I attended the retreat in Switzerland, Florida, swatting mosquitoes and feeling dead in the water. At this point in my life, I had completed my second year in the U.S. Coast Guard as a Marine Inspector/Investigator, and I was still unmarried. I continued to be troubled by my conflicting feelings which had contributed to two broken relationships. I was mourning my friend and classmate, Lincoln McCarthy, who had often spoken of becoming a priest before his tragic death. I was anguishing over the unexpected death of another friend, Jon Lieberman.

The three-day retreat centered around the suffering, death and resurrection of Jesus. On the last night of the weekend, I walked outside under the wonderful live oak trees. There was the full moon. It shone just as bright and glorious as it had twice before.

I refused to look away almost in defiance. God was calling me clearly like the siren's call to change course. God wasn't going to tell me if I should be a priest. He simply conveyed in a mysterious and very whispered but firm way that I should enter the seminary and start a wonderful journey. I decided at that moment I would give the seminary two years of my life. I wasn't convinced I would make it. Believe me, there are other candidates much more inclined to this vocation. And even now, I look at myself sometimes in disbelief that I am still a priest. I was given so much, and I felt the need to deliver the cargo of love. The Kings Point fight song goes, "We can cross any ocean, sail any river, give us the goods and we'll deliver. Damn the submarines! We're the men of the Merchant Marines!"

It wasn't that I lacked preparation for this next step in my journey. The Coast Guard motto is: ***Semper Paratus*** *(Always Prepared).* I was just really scared, insecure, and immature, not knowing where this journey would take me. Part of me thought if I didn't pursue a career as a ship's officer or at least in the maritime field that it would be cheating the American people out of the cost of my education. What did a degree in nautical science have to do with being a priest?

In August, 1984, I left active duty in the Coast Guard and entered a seminary in St. Meinrad. While at the seminary, I was attached to the Marine Safety Office in Louisville, Kentucky, as a Coast Guard reservist. I had never attended Catholic school and was pretty intimidated upon my initial arrival at the seminary. I would give the seminary a two-year try. If this was my path, ordination into the priesthood would take five or six years.

After taking pre-Theology courses at St. Meinrad, I transferred to St. Vincent de Paul Regional Seminary in Boynton Beach, Florida, where I earned a Masters of Art in Theology and a Masters of Divinity. I remained a Reservist at the Marine Safety Detachment in Fort Pierce for two more years and then focused on my studies at the seminary full time. I resigned my commission in the Coast Guard and took the oath as a Naval Reserve Officer in the Chaplain Candidate Program in January, 1987. That summer, I attended the Chaplain Basic School in Newport, Rhode Island. I would be known as a chaplain candidate for the next four years, spending 35 days a year on active duty to fulfill my reserve requirements. My places of duty included NAS Hospital Jacksonville, Naval Recruit Training Orlando, the USS Lexington, and Mayport Naval Station. On May 19, 1990, I was at last ordained a priest for the Diocese of St. Augustine. My first assignment was next to the Mayport Naval Station. So in July of that year, as a priest and a chaplain candidate, I filled in for the priest on the base for 35 days of active duty.

That was the year Desert Storm started. Usually, one must have been a priest for three years before going on active duty as a chaplain. During war, however, rules change. Out of fear of being recalled, I withheld my paperwork to become a full chaplain. I definitely did not want to go to Kuwait or Iraq or anywhere in the Middle East. The thought was terrifying to me. Back in the Academy days while on my sea year, our second ship had pulled into Ashdod and Haifa in Israel. I visited Jerusalem with the help of a Muslim tour guide; he showed me the wall around the city, the Dome of the Rock, the Holy Sepulcher, and the Wailing Wall. After my return to the ship on a gorgeous day, a bomb exploded at the Tel Aviv bus stop where we had stood just minutes before. I had good reasons to be afraid of the Middle East.

During the summer of 1993, my bishop recommended I go on active duty. I was stunned. I had "toyed" with the idea of becoming an active duty priest chaplain, but I really didn't want to leave the area. I thought going on active duty was a terrible idea. I gave the bishop many reasons why I felt this way. The bishop insisted, however, because of my experience and because of Jacksonville's position as a "Navy" town. Bishops are usually reluctant to let their priests go on active duty when the priest requests it.

I would most likely be assigned to a Marine unit in Okinawa, Japan, and I was afraid of the physical requirements and a grunt's tough life in the field. Deep in my heart, the idea of going on active duty was actually exciting, but my heart and mind weren't in synchronization. Just six months later, January of 1994, I flew to Okinawa to serve with the Marines. Upon arrival, I was attached to the Stinger Battery, the grunts of the air. My first week there, I stood in the middle of a field on Camp Fuetemna and complained loudly to the wind, "What am I doing here?"

The U.S. Marines would help me with that one. Their motto is simply, ***"Semper Fidelis"*** (Always Faithful). I was being asked to be faithful to *'the CALL.'*

Suddenly, I remembered the quote I had created for my page in the Academy's yearbook in 1981:

'If you do instead of complain, you will complain a lot less.'

I was complaining and I realized it. I was actually whining, which was even worse. We complained and whined a lot at Kings Point even though our time there was a true blessing.

At that moment, I decided to live up to our motto of ***"Acta non Verba."*** A month later, I received orders to serve with the grunts in Camp Fuji, Japan. In the middle of the dreary winter, it was tough to avoid complaining when celebrating the sacraments in the field with all that snow, mud, dirt and grunting!

After completing sixteen months in Okinawa, I was transferred to Roosevelt Roads in Puerto Rico. Before my departure, the Marines awarded me the Navy/Marine Corps Commendation Medal for my work there, including co-creating an innovative suicide awareness program for the Marines. It was presented to about 2,000 Marines and Sailors. However, my greatest treasure wasn't an award at all.

I would participate in strenuous humps with the Stinger Battery and rise at zero-dark-thirty to run with them five days a week. I joked and complained about the scars on my feet from the many blisters and escapades of living in the field and running all the time. On the last day I was to run with the Stinger Battery, we did the daily seven, which usually totaled nineteen exercises. Go figure! However, the Captain informed us we were to run around the whole flight line. I panicked. I knew that route was over nine miles. I figured I could run three miles or six maximum, but not nine. At the time, I thought the age of 36 was too old for this! I felt my calves begin to tighten. I approached the Captain and expressed my concern that I might not be able to make it. He asked if I was complaining. We were the same rank, so I responded with, "Maybe." He replied very loudly, "Chaplain Camarda! If you don't run around this flight line with us, I am going to drag your @#$!! around!" All of the Marines heard this.

I have no idea how I ran around that flight line. I could barely stand after finishing the nine miles. I was more than ready to leave the Marines and be done with them at this point. They formed up as usual after morning PT, just as the sun began to get really warm. I stood brooding in the back row, and the Captain barked out, "Chaplain Camarda! Front and center." I made my way forward and was presented with a most touching plaque that read:

Padre Camarda
A Stinger Marine in
Spirit, Mind, Heart and Scars!

Marines love their chaplains. What I discovered is that it is kind of Scriptural. If a chaplain "pitches his tent" among the Marines, they enter into a deeper faith with God. I have been humbled more than once in my life. I suspect I will be humbled many more times.

My next two years were at Naval Station, Roosevelt Roads in Puerto Rico with three months at Guantanamo Bay, Cuba, during the Haitian and Cuban crisis in 1995. In the winter of 1997, I left active duty and returned to my diocese. From 1999 until August of 2004, I was the acting pastor for St. Patrick's, an inner-city parish and school in Jacksonville. I felt truly called to this ministry. Then, the Navy ordered me to Iraq.

Those seven years before Iraq translated into much complaining and whining. I was once again emotionally fragile as I had been before my graduation from Kings Point. **I was afraid.**

During this time, I wrote an essay called *"Why Am I a Priest Today?"* The essay was published in the Emmanuel Magazine in September, 2001. By sharing this, I hope to help many of us in our wrestling with God, as the wrestling simulates the ups and downs of our spiritual journeys.

I have had a very colorful past, practically sailing around the world. God is so real to me. It's as if I am continually on the verge of bursting, but I don't. In my heart, I knew I was a priest before I was ordained May 19, 1990. There was nothing I could do to stop this process (God's call), including girls, engagement, economic security, job satisfaction, or the deep need for children from my loins.

For many years, I begged God to tell me clearly and distinctly if he wanted me as his priest. God never answered me directly. In fact, when I was silent and listened, God was mute. When I sailed the seas as a cadet, he shouted and sang. God has only spoken to me once. I still cry when I recall it.

My friend, Jon, shot himself in the head and died. I was told by religious people he could not go to heaven and would most likely experience hell because he was an atheist or agnostic. What kind of God was that?

At that time, I was a Coast Guard officer. The day after I received the news, I reported to work as usual. My commanding officer commented that I looked like my best friend had just died. "He did," I responded, as cold and unfeeling as I could reply. Jon had been my roommate at the Merchant Marine Academy, my friend who had listened attentively after my fiancée dumped me. Jon was my friend in Cocoa Beach when I traveled from Jacksonville once or twice a week. We spoke into the night. We talked about God. Jon was manic depressive, but I never realized it. No one had told me, not even Jon. God hadn't told me. Why couldn't I have been there for my friend when he was in the hospital? Why couldn't I have been able to hold him, love him, and tell him I loved him?

The pain was deep, so deep. It went beyond loneliness and betrayal. It struck at the core of belief…of love.

So I stumbled into a small chapel where I had shared broken bread and poured out Jesus' blood. Only twenty or thirty people were at Mass, and I was very late. Almost as soon as I arrived, we stood for the Lord's Prayer. A woman reached for my hand and squeezed. The tears suddenly fell as they fall now in writing this, only more fell then. I was taken by surprise at my own outburst and sobbing. I was inconsolable. As I moved forward, trembling, to receive the Lord of Life in my hands and then on my tongue, I was very hungry for something, I was thirsting, but for what I didn't know. I continued to cry and weep like the woman at Jesus' feet…aching for acceptance, love, and the need to give love.

With no one left in the chapel and all but a trace of energy gone, I approached the altar of God, fell to my knees, and uttered the most honest prayer of my life. "Let him know I love him." My prayer was filled with genuine emotion. The only direct words from God I have ever heard or expect to hear were about to be given to me. The warmth of God's arms surrounded me, and the words were whispered into my ear, "He knows, Ron. He knows."

God never told me directly to become a priest or to even become a minister. God loved me into service, into the priesthood. There are many better candidates than me, but I accepted the call to follow. And I said, "Here I am; use me." Many times, I have cried since that November of 1982. I question God. I wrestle and feel great pain for the many people who don't know our loving, tender, merciful, fun God. I have been betrayed and slandered by colleagues and parishioners, and I have plunged into dark nights of loneliness and doubt. I have angered myself when I feared embracing a person with AIDS as he was sweating. I need not doubt God's love. I have more to go. When the dying hold my hand, they grip my heart as well. I feel the pull into the dark grave. My faith tells me God will raise me up, all of us up.

I have been disappointed with the institutional aspect of the church when rules have priority over people. Jesus wouldn't put up with it, yet in some ways I go with the flow. For those times, I am deeply sorry. God knows how to love. Yet we have continuously forgotten.

This is why I am called to be God's mouthpiece, God's priest: To tell of his love, her love, their love. God has blessed me with all the tools I need, including intimate friends, passion, and compassion. God even gives me strength and courage to bend the rules occasionally. We are God's lovers, and we must give it *all* away. We must be bread to the hungry at our doors. We must lavish the hungry with the plenty we have known in the Word of God, Jesus.

Go ahead and look into the eyes of the poor, the hungry, the suffering and the dying. Their eyes are the windows of heaven. My life has never been the same since God spoke to me, healed me, and loved me through the poor in spirit.

God loves me, and I will follow him through this life and into eternity. There have been times when I reluctantly went to another parish or assignment across the world. But I have always encountered love and God. Sometimes, I encountered God in the freezing rain or the sweltering heat of the field, while my feet experienced serious scars. Sometimes, I felt God in maximum security, with three murderers needing my eyes to return back to Him. Once, I encountered God while staying all night in an emergency room with a little girl who had jumped from an eight-story building. I held her hand and pleaded with God for her life… and my prayer was answered. Another time, it was holding a man who lost his wife during childbirth, and not knowing what to say.

How does one explain Sarah, who, at 84 and deaf, holds my hand, looks into my eyes and reads my lips? How does the heart contain the Cuban migrants who trust me and say 'Amen' to my challenges to love and forgive?

Imagine two mothers of six-month-old babies together for baptism. Both babies were in trouble at birth; both mothers were mad at God. The potential for permanent damage angered and scared them. They could not understand their feelings until the feast of the Holy Family, when I plunged both children into the baptismal waters and raised them up as an offering to God. The baptisms were a great source of healing for these mothers.

Maria and Angel renewed their vows after 50 years of marriage. In my poorer than average Spanish, I received their love and unleashed God's blessings. Angel was ill, but in front of all to witness, the moment was one of healthy radiance. Angel died a month later.

Even when I break from priestly duties, I vacation with God and my friend. We have had so much fun visiting the missions in California and New Mexico. I walked the way of the cross in Jerusalem and passed through the garden of Gethsemane. I cruised through the Panama Canal and climbed to the top of Mount Fuji and to the bottom of the Grand Canyon.

As for priestly things, I have presided at Easter Vigils and sung the *Exultet.* I have held the hands of the very old and the very young before death took them away, only to touch me much deeper in the mystery of God…of love that is stronger than death.

Celebrating Mass with the holy sisters of Calcutta, the Missionaries of Charity, is total peace, total love, and total service. Healing the sick of mind, heart and body is awesome. Teaching the children to touch the elderly, sing to them, play with them, and adopt them is sheer joy. Holding the lonely, comforting the sorrowful, and understanding the angry all cause me to lose myself in Jesus. I am but an instrument to be played over and over again.

Before I was ordained, a street person suffering with schizophrenia once gave me a dirty recorder/flute and asked me to play it. Over and over again, I played that instrument for the sick, the depressed, and the confused. We are all instruments of God's love and grace; we only need to learn how to play the tunes and experience the love.

God is so awesome and cannot be contained in our narrow or limited perceptions. God is love; a Love that creates and permeates every fiber of our existence. God flies, God swims, and God struggles to love us in ways that we will recognize Him.

We are God's body and blood, God's flesh. "Yahweh's love will last forever; his faithfulness to the end of time. Yahweh is a loving God. Yahweh is the faithful one."

So why am I a priest today? Being a priest is my opportunity to give back to God a fraction of the blessings God has showered on me. Nothing less than every breath, touch, and hope belongs to this God of love who has never let me down. I followed because Jesus called me, unworthy as I am.

1 October 2004 — Camp Fallujah, Iraq

Even before the Navy deployed me to Iraq, I knew in my soul God was going to challenge me to be more intentional in my priesthood. I would be called to something much deeper than I have ever experienced. Jesus asked me to put out into deep water and lower my nets for a catch. I instinctively protested that I was hard at work at my ministry. (I believed I was a pretty good fisher of men and women).

In reality, **I was afraid** to be with Ron. I was afraid to be with myself. My emotions got the best of me. Even my homilies (sermons) were filled with emotions that were all over the place.

Nothing in my life could have prepared me for the bludgeoning and tearing apart of flesh by improvised explosive devices (IED's). Thousands of rockets and mortars launched into our camp create a surreal environment. In addition to my duties as chaplain to Bravo Surgical Company, the senior chaplains call upon me to minister Catholic Sacraments to the entire base and also to the Regiment in the field and satellite camps. During the height of the surge into the city of Fallujah, it is estimated there will be over 10,000 troops in the area. I hesitate, out of fear, to go forward into the city every Sunday to celebrate Mass and "pitch my tent" with those risking their lives for our freedoms.

I must pilot the ship of my soul with precision and great trust in God. Mother Theresa of Calcutta taught me to celebrate every Mass as if it were my first Mass, my only Mass, and my last Mass. This serves me well with the real possibility of death always a few yards away in Iraq. There are many truly genuine heroes and heroines out here. Many of the troops, including non-Catholics, call me "Father." I love the Marines, soldiers and sailors entrusted to me. My heart breaks with every bludgeoned person, amputation, broken spirit, KIA, and casualty.

Truth be told, I am not convinced we should be in this war. However, I came because when our soldiers, Marines or sailors are here because of their oaths to our nation, they deserve all of our support. I have been blessed with an incredible education, journey through the seas of life, and wisdom. I must deliver the goods, despite the hideous crimes of terrorists and insurrectionists. Actions speak louder than words. The political environment and the fog of war are beyond me. Humanity is the most precious cargo and needs to be shipped with great love, courage, honor, strength and commitment. I am here to deliver the gifts given to me, the cargo once delivered to me in the Mariners Chapel at the U.S. Merchant Marine Academy back in 1977.

Acta non Verba! *Deeds not Words!*

Padre Camarda relaxes in front of Bravo Surgical Hospital before "running" over to the gym to rejoice in PT (physical training). Notice my smile before PT!

Chapter VI
OCTOBER in FALLUJAH

By the time October rolled around, there was a buildup for the Battle of Fallujah. No one really knew exactly when it would happen. There was an average of 1000 rockets or mortars sent into the camp each month. Since I did not carry a weapon, my Religious Program Specialist (RP) First Class Petty Officer, Patrick Bowen, was basically my bodyguard. Patrick set up for Masses and was my computer guru. When casualties arrived, Patrick also worked in the reception area. When bloody uniforms were stripped off incoming patients, Patrick assisted by determining the individual's religious preference. Often, the dog tag would reveal clues to the member's faith. However, "no preference" was common and almost always the case for Jewish troops. I could understand.

Whenever I went out to the forward operating bases (FOB's) or into the heart of the city, Patrick was close by my side. I was very blessed to have this man. He took his job very seriously and ensured my protection. Our political views and denominations were different; he was Methodist, and I was a Catholic priest. His tastes of music and food were not the same as mine. However, I loved Patrick and depended on him. We had loneliness in common since we were the only reservists in the company.

Our time went by quickly since we were not confined to the base camp, and there was so much work to do. We were always on the go. Often, we woke earlier than others and climbed into our sleeping bags long after them. We averaged nine Masses on weekends and one every day. We tried to take off each Monday which was successful about fifty percent of the time. Patrick was great about setting up and breaking down Mass in the field. He often secured transportation, and that was a challenge. We always had to go in convoy with a brief before every movement.

I had gotten in the habit of praying in the back of the hospital immediately after the 8:00 a.m. staff meetings. I sat in a plastic chair between the building and a huge cement blockade around the hospital. I brought my prayer book and a cup of coffee and spent about an hour just praying or writing. Most of what I wrote in my journal was done in that little haven. It surely wasn't romantic. At first, it was extremely hot, and I squeezed myself into the last bits of shade. Then, the weather turned cold, but I desperately needed this place of quiet. The dentist and operating room machines were nearby and often made concentration difficult. However, there were a couple of plants and every once in awhile, a bird. I honestly do not know how these plants survived in the arid and severe weather. Patrick knew my prayer spot and could reach me in case of an emergency. Actually, most of the company knew about my haven. There were a few times I was called for incoming casualties. However, there just seemed to be very few casualties at that particular time each day. During the Al Fajr (coded name for

"The Battle for Fallujah"), my morning prayer was impossible, but I did manage alternate times throughout the day.

Pock marks in the blockade belied the relative peace of my sacred space. Less than ten feet from my prayer place, an army major medical doctor and a sergeant had been killed instantly back in March of that year. A mortar had exploded while the doctor was talking on a satellite phone to his wife, the mother of his children. The danger was real. Even prayer was a risky endeavor.

First Class Religious Program Specialist (RP1) Patrick Bowen, USNR

Instrument of Peace!

4 October 2004 **A Talk with God**

You knew, O Beloved Lord, better than I what was to unfold yesterday. You had me in your arms as I wrestled, whimpered, cried and sadly…complained.

Transportation was a mess as I attempted to provide Catholic services to the camps outside Camp Fallujah. I am sorry, Lord; I may have been irritated and slightly ugly. But all along you had me in your love, even though you may have been disappointed with me. My homily was about faith, and I exhibited little faith, if any. And that is the problem. It wasn't my homily; it was yours: your stories, your parables, your suffering and your death. I did nothing for I am a servant, unprofitable at that, of your Word, your Love, your hopes, your dreams, and your commands.

Yesterday was for me. My inconveniences and frustrations were all gifts. I see this now; the purpose was to bring me and draw me closer to your heart.

Forgive me, Lord, for doubting. Forgive me for my harsh words and my insane stubbornness. I knew it was a graced moment when Captain Brian Heatherman invited me to the infamous Abu Ghraib prison. It was you, more than me, who desired and wanted your Body to be sacrificed there. I didn't trust you. I feel so goofy, almost ashamed. And yet I know within my soul and heart, that you desire not that I be ashamed or embarrassed. I will profit immensely if I simply follow you and fill my being with you – Love itself.

O Beloved, you are mightier than the storms of hatred and insanity. It is You, and You alone, who will bring peace and stability to this region of the world. It is You who is already at work in every darkened heart, fulfilling Your promise given here almost 4,000 years ago.

Awesome! Lord Jesus, my spirit, life, and breath; I beg of You to show me Your plan so I can better follow You into Eternity.

What a story last night. You placed me in the center of those men, Baptists and Protestants, to lead them in the Word of God. I felt their mistrust, but I knew You placed me there. About 25 men gathered for the non-denominational prayer service. Chaplain Ron Kennedy was very sick, and You urged me to be uncomfortable and cover for him. When I proclaimed Your Word, the authority was there. I felt it. When You spoke to them through me, I was in awe. I'm not sure You wanted me to lay hands on them, though, because some of them got up and scattered at that! Suspicious I presume of the Anti-Christ and us 'Catholics.'

What must You have endured when Your very own people got up and abandoned You as you gave them Your body, Your blood, and Your heart? Come to think of it, I still do this. You say to me, "And you, Ron Moses, are you going to leave me, too?" I fumble with words, "O not me, for You Jesus have the words of Eternal Life." And yet, You know me so well. I will choose death over and over until I surrender not just my will, but my very life and breath.

O Jesus, what have You done? There are so many holier priests than me. How could you pick me when these men and women will be experiencing life-changing amputations, wounds or even dying?

I want to trust You totally, Jesus. Increase my faith! Increase my love!

And whatever you ask in My name, that I will do,
that the Father may be glorified in the Son.
John 14:13

You ask, "What do you want Me to do for you?"

I say, "Increase my love for You and my neighbor and enemy. Increase my love. Increase my love."

And the Word became flesh and dwelt among us. God suffered, died and has been raised from the dead. And we will all Rise Again!"

Teach me patience, Lord, Beloved, Holy One.

Teach me wisdom…

Teach me Love.

I love you,

Ron Moses +

I can do all things through Christ who strengthens me.
Philippians 4:13

Dusty back corner of the clinic
Yet life giving
I first notice the shadows on the barriers
A mimosa type tree and palm bush
  Leading my eyes to the real
Two birds, rather pretty
      Black crown, white face alight turn,
Flies annoying, full of life, closing in on my eyes
Blue sky wrestling with rising dust; brownish blue of sunlight
Pretty, delicate wind
  Colors of browns showing signs of distinction
Life in a war zone
  Rockets in, rockets out
    Life goes on
Prayers amidst the rubble
  Allah, God, Yahweh
        Be praised ----
Who shall win?
Lover of enemies
Lovers of enemies
Blast us with Your love
Blast us with Your healing
  Pretty flowers
  Pretty trees
  Pretty neat
  Pretty cool.

Bless the Lord, sing songs of Creation
Instruments of peace and love!

6 October 2004 — Bravo Surgical: Fallujah, Iraq

I am exhausted; something left me, yet something remains in me. I am back "home" after my journey, our journey to the infamous Abu Ghraib Prison and the Marines of Lima Company. What a place!

The camp itself had a bad spiritual odor. Images of post World War II and the subsequent rubble filled my eyes and nostrils as I choked within and gagged. I wanted to say, "Why me?" But, in my growing patience and impatience, I am increasingly aware of the Master's will in me. God cares. That is all we really need to know. God loves. God heals. And God wills.

Again, in my pride, I can scarcely admit that I thought I was there to offer services like Mass. What I discovered is that we (the clergy) have grossly neglected the People of God. I reflect on how inadequate my spiritual formation was growing up, and now I see face-to-face the resulting atrocities of a life without training in love – love in the likeness and compassion of Jesus.

Many, if not most, men are fatherless and motherless. The burdensome anxieties of generations are passed down, piling up and burying all life. We tend to blame anyone and everyone else, as long as we don't have to question ourselves.

At the prison, insurrectionists attempt to send rockets into the walls to release their people. Too much violence, too much miscalculation, too much hatred exists.

In our country, shattered lives constitute the masses; divorce, abuse, addictions and ignorance abound in the majority of people. And so, our nation is crumbling from within. Only God can save, and yet we have not disciplined ourselves or our children to suffer, to die and to rise again. We must look inward.

I rode in a Humvee through the streets of Iraq. I wore armor to protect my flesh from shrapnel, snipers and even anger. But I was not protected from the shrapnel and the casualty of my soul. How many orphans did I see? How many unemployed men? How many widowed women who witnessed their husbands or children decapitated or their homes stolen or destroyed?

I returned "home" without a scratch, but the vehicle of my soul was totaled. I walked out unharmed but permanently changed. I haven't the words to express it. Denial wells deep within me. My joy seems lost this morning, lost in a land of faith mingled with the blood of many centuries. Brother against brother, father against son, daughter against mother, and on and on. Nothing can separate us from the love of God who chooses us above his Son. How long, Father, will you love us in this manner? Will you ever grow weary of our inept behavior? Is the door closing? Are we okay? How do you still love us?

So weak, so intolerant, and so selfish we are. Rescue us, O Beloved, from our fears and ourselves. Enkindle again within us the fire and compassion and the forgiveness of your love. Forge it. Enforce it. And be deaf to our whining and complaining. Rescue us and mold us into your image so that we may be enslaved no more. Lord, have mercy, for we have sinned.

I love you, Ron Moses +

For I, the Lord your God will hold your right hand, saying to you, "Fear not, I will help you." – Isaiah 41:13

And then late this evening around 11:00 p.m., the mail delivery convoy was hit by an IED. The soldiers were bringing mail to troops at various locations within the Anbar Province of Iraq. I anointed Ryan Hobbs, a Catholic. Tony Edwards, a Presbyterian and the father of three children, needed surgery. Jessica Cawvey, a non-denominational Christian, was pronounced dead. Jessica was the first and only female servicemember who died at Bravo Surgical.

They were only delivering the mail.

7 October 2004 **I am 45 today!**

I woke up this morning feeling a little blue and achy. Throughout the day, I reflected on being 45. It honestly seems that 35 was only yesterday. I have lived a wonderful life filled with gratitude and joy.

Last night, while the clock passed midnight into this day, I ministered to three Army soldiers who were pummeled by shrapnel from an IED. Ryan's face was diced up and had many serious cuts. The staff sergeant, Tony, suffered painful wounds to his body. Jessica arrived dead.

Ryan was rather quickly sedated… so much blood from the face. Tony is the father of three of his own children, yet he exhibited true fatherly concern for his troops. Two casualties were sent to other places.

Sometimes, I distract the wounded from their pain as I talk to them. This possibly helps to distract me from my own pain. Oh, well. It doesn't seem like this would be tough work, but it is. I have to be Christ not only to the sick and wounded, but also to those who bring them in and to those who do the healing. I constantly observe eyes and body language. It is fascinating and intense. Many in the ward are Catholic by name but struggling in their faith.

Today, I went to the chaplain office, and I was all alone. And then came another mortar rocket after all the warnings, when it was supposedly all clear… Boom! Crack!

I fell to the floor, attempting to hide beneath the desk for just a moment, and then I was off. Eventually, I looked and saw a man lying on the ground with blood surrounding him. I was less than fifty yards away from contact. I thought the man was likely Baptist, yet he looked vaguely familiar. When the ambulance arrived, I ran to Bravo Surgical since I knew the injured man would soon be there. I arrived before the ambulance.

Charles was from Trinidad…and Catholic. Blood oozed from his shattered eardrum. When I was a baby, a hurricane caused my eardrum to burst. Here, the blast did it. I flourished when my eardrum burst, because it then revealed an undetected interior swelling and infection on my brain which was then treated. Forty-four years later, here I am.

Another arrived who had probably been knocked unconscious. His name was David, and he couldn't remember anything. This was probably a good thing. It is so easy to forget we are at war zone. Just the other day, I observed children playing in this modern war zone that is Iraq.

Charles, a staff sergeant, needed water to swish in his mouth. After bringing him water, I told him to just spit it out into the cup. He missed the cup and soaked my hand and arm with chew and saliva. Poor guy was shocked he "got" the priest! I was okay with it, really!

I then went to the head, and tears and intense emotions welled up inside me and to the surface again. But I'm not erupting…yet.

God be merciful to me, a sinner.

I love You. Thank you, God, for another year of me!

Prayer in the Field

I was ordained a deacon one year before I was ordained a priest. At that time, I promised my Bishop I would pray the Liturgy of Hours. This is a prayer book often done in community, but we Diocesan priests pray it often by ourselves. I have really grown to love this prayer that encompasses Sacred Scripture and prayers throughout the day. There are four volumes and special prayers for every day of the year. This prayer helped to anchor me in Iraq. It kind of boosted me for the day. My friend, a priest in Gainesville, Florida, asked me to look back on the prayers for August 13. I found the following excerpts:

> *We are warriors now, fighting on the battlefield of faith, and God sees all we do; the angels watch and so does Christ.*
>
> - *What honor and glory and joy, to do battle in the presence of God, and to have Christ approve our victory.*
>
> *Let us arm ourselves in full strength and prepare ourselves for the ultimate struggle with blameless hearts, true faith and unyielding courage.*
>
> - *What honor and glory and joy, to do battle in the presence of God, and to have Christ approve our victory.*

I willingly boast of my weakness, that the power of Christ may rest upon me. Therefore I am content with weakness, with mistreatment, with distress, with persecutions and difficulties for the sake of Christ; for when I am powerless, it is then that I am strong.

– 2 Corinthians 12:9-10

Let us pray:

Father, when your son was handed over to torture and seemed abandoned by you, he cried out to you from the cross and death was destroyed, life was restored. By his death and resurrection, may we see the day when the poor person is saved, the downtrodden is lifted up and the chains that bind people are broken. United to the thanks that Christ gives you, your Church will sing your praises.

I include Scripture passages, writings of the Church and Saints, and prayers in my journal. They are woven throughout the book. These elements were important because the words and prayers strengthened me for the horrors and tears I encountered, often before they even happened. Sometimes, the words served to strengthen my despairing spirit.

After copying these prayers into my journal, I then wrote from my heart and soul. In this passage, I vacillated between praying to Jesus and talking to myself. It helped me make observations and clarify my own needs.

The Eyes of Prayer

Thank You, Lord Jesus, for my eyes. I see more and more through your heart. O the eyes of others, for them I give grateful praise. How often we turn away when eyes fill up with something more than water, more than tears. O how we can communicate with our faces, our whole bodies, our entire beings.

Here, so far from home, I am comfortable contemplating. I have so much more than most. Sure, I have food and shelter. Yet, faith is my true rock, protection and security.

Prayer is exciting and is food for my soul. Prayer is not a chore; it is more important than food, even water. There have been moments in my life when I could actually taste love, so full, so detached. Fleeting, yes, but gripping. For forty days before her death, my mother ate nothing. Yet, although her body was ravished and depleted, she looked fully satisfied, energized and peaceful. O how I long to be done with food, clothing and shelter. How I long to be free of this worldly attachment. As my spiritual body matures, my physical body steadily deteriorates. Yet it is this physical body, this gift, from which my spirit and my being feeds. We eat the Body and drink the Blood of our Creator… this mingles with our own body…until no fragments remain. Eucharist is truly incredible.

Jesus once said, "Do not be afraid of those who can hurt or destroy the body. Be afraid of the One who can take our soul, the Creator. Fear the Lord and you will experience the Love of the Lord."

Following the death of Martha's brother, Lazarus, consoled her by saying, "I am the Resurrection and the life. Whoever believes in me and dies will live. And whoever <u>lives</u> and <u>believes</u> will never die. Do you believe this?"

Martha said, and I say, "Yes, my Lord!"

"Yes, my Lord!"

"Yes, my Lord!"

Here I am, Lord. I come to do your will.

9 October 2004 Saturday

This was an eerie and frightening night. Seven Marines from 3/1 Battalion arrived at the hospital with mysterious burns to their faces, hands and eyes. The emergency docs couldn't figure out the source of the burns. As the chaplain, I was emotionally torn. I couldn't say everything would be alright because I wasn't sure. My gut felt as if it was on the floor. Some of the men had difficulty breathing so my breathing technique was not helpful. Were the men's injuries the result of a gas bomb? Had they inadvertently contaminated the hospital? In the coming days, they would remain in the ward for weeks. One or two were medically evacuated. Our little hospital was similar to the movie and television show, *M.A.S.H.* The Marines who stayed in the ward didn't return to their units for such a long time. The lengthy hospital stay provided them with much time to think. This wasn't necessarily a good thing in a war zone.

13 October 2004 **Wednesday**

Happy Birthday to the United States Navy – 229 Years!

I was asked to pray at the Navy Birthday Ball. Of course it wasn't a true ball but a small celebration in the desert with a birthday cake, parading of the colors and pomp. For some reason, we call this a "Ball." Many Marines would attend the ceremony. Since the Navy was actually a minority, it would have to be sharp.

When a chaplain prays at these types of events, the prayer must be generic and inclusive. This is a great challenge today with such diversity in faiths. In preparation, I researched various military prayer books and adapted them for the situation. This was my prayer:

Blessed are you, the alpha and the omega of our faith, for you called us out of darkness into your marvelous light. You enabled the blind to see, the deaf to hear. Help our unbelief.

Lord, keep us in your love, preserve our community – do not let us be separated from one another.

Give us strength in temptation, endurance in trial, and gratitude in prosperity.

Most of us call the Mystery in our life something like:

Yahweh	*I AM*	*Silence*
God	*Great Spirit*	*Consoler*
Allah	*Father*	*Mother*
Nature	*Lord*	*Jesus*
Beloved	*Creator*	*Love*
In God we Trust		

In the Navy we are always in awe at the immensity, the awe, the danger, and the magnificence of the seas and the oceans. Like the Siren's call, we are called to consider the spiritual. I invite you all to listen to this song as I sing it and use your word for the Mystery when it is God...

All creatures of our God and King,
Lift up your voice and with us sing, Alleluia! Alleluia!
Thou burning sun with golden beam
Thou silver moon with softer gleam
O praise God, O praise God
Alleluia! Alleluia! Alleluia!

Thou rushing winds that are so strong,
Ye clouds that sail in heaven along
O praise God, O praise God
Thou rising morn in praise rejoice
Ye lights of evening find a voice!
O praise God, O praise God
Alleluia! Alleluia! Alleluia!

Let us pray:

Eternal Lord God, you alone spread out the heavens and rule the raging sea. Take into your most gracious protection our country's Navy and all who serve therein. Preserve them from the dangers of the sea and from the violence of the enemy, that they may be a safeguard unto the United States of America, a security for such as sail upon the seas in peaceful and lawful missions. Thank you, O God, may our sailors serve their country and give grateful praise to All Creation.

Then I played Taps on my tiny recorder that sounds a little like bagpipes and then read the words.

Thanks and praise...

14 October 2004 Thursday ~ St. Callistus

Callistus was a slave before becoming a son of God. God set Callistus free, and this freedom then cut his life short. No one could give his life without believing there is life and glory beyond. Faith is not knowing for sure, yet still making the sacrifice.

Here I am

Lost in the desert

Swatting flies

Dodging rockets and mortars and

Gruesome and diabolical injuries

From human to human,

Here I am

Knowing that I am insignificant

And unprofitable both,

Love creates the hidden me

Fashioned in the image of God

Disease causes me to hold on to the people, possessions,

power and pleasures of this passing world.

Jesus draws me into the desert.

My desires that are not pure at all,

motivate me to follow.

Ancient Mesopotamia

Like yesterday to God

Still fighting

Brother against brother, sister against sister.

Why don't we listen?

What stops our growth into peace and civility?

What parts do we, as a country play?

Without reflection on our participation in the conflict,

we will never be at peace.

Every prophet warned us

Let go! Let go! Let go of possessions, power, and pleasures!

Embrace the poor, the oppressed, the blind, and the misguided!

Forgive those who hurt you while they are still hurting you.

Trust in the love of God.

Share the wealth of Jesus welling up to eternal life.

The more we give, the stronger the current of love

The more we hold on, the more we will be flooded with death, danger, and disaster

Love my people

And you will live forever

Thus says the Lord!

For the Lord is good: his mercy is everlasting,

And his truth endures to all generations.

– Psalm 100:5

15 October 2004 PFC Oscar A. Martinez, USMC

On October 12, a mortar killed a Marine who arrived in Iraq less than a month ago. The memorial service was today at 4 pm. I attended the service to support the Marines who knew him. Oscar was only 19 years old. When Oscar's mother was struck with cancer, he became the man of the house. He cared for his younger siblings. The Marine Corps likely provided the strength and discipline Oscar might have lacked in his family of origin.

I gleaned a few things about Oscar from his friends who spoke at the memorial service. Oscar smiled, laughed, and thoroughly enjoyed the life given to him but now, his life has abruptly ended. Over 300 Marines gathered to show gratitude for Oscar's sacrifice. In many ways, the whole ceremony reminded me of Good Friday services when we remember the death of Jesus of Nazareth.

The Scripture at the memorial service was from the book of Qoheleth (Ecclesiastes) and spoke of vanity of vanities in which there is a time for everything, including a time to be born and a time to die. The Gospel spoke of the many houses God will provide, one for each of us. Jesus loves us and assures us.

A huge Marine Corps flag, approximately thirty feet by twenty, draped the stage. The flag has a red background and a globe with an anchor in the center. Above the globe, and eagle touts "Semper Fidelis." Underneath this motto is a banner of "The United States Marine Corps." There were also seven Marine Corps flags and one U.S. Navy flag on stands that fanned out.

At the stage's center was the cross equivalent. There was no body. Oscar's boots were there. His rifle also stood beside the boots and supported his helmet and dangling dog tags.

The words and benediction were spoken. The gunny sergeant then marched to the front and called the roll. The names of about five Marines in Oscar's platoon were called. These Marines forcefully proclaimed with a trace of guarded grief, "Present!"

Then the Gunny yelled,

"Private First Class Martinez!"

only silence

"Private First Class Oscar Martinez!"

only silence

"PRIVATE FIRST CLASS OSCAR A. MARTINEZ, UNITED STATES MARINE CORPS!!!"

still silent

Then the Gunny barked,

"Private First Class Oscar A. Martinez,

United States Marine Corps,

Killed in Action by enemy attack,

October 12, 2004"

The Gunny saluted and then… TAPS.

After filing up, over three hundred of us, one by one, gave Oscar our respect and love. The tribute was very much like Good Friday when we individually go forward to the cross. It was emotional and tearful. I will never again experience Good Friday without remembering this service. Jesus had a cross rather than a rifle. Jesus has conquered and will eventually gather us all home. God is Good! All the time!

PFC Oscar A. Martinez, USMC

19 October 2004 **Tuesday ~ Fallujah, Iraq**

"Reflecting on Sunday"

Marcous laid on a stretcher in the trauma room. His fellow Marine, Sean, was beside him on another stretcher. Marcous' eyes were bright blue and green: alive; however, his body was full of shrapnel. Sean had lost a great deal of blood, and his legs were in grave danger of being amputated. These two Marines had only come into the Main Camp to call home and to relax at the exchange. A mortar hit only a few meters behind their truck and pierced its heavy armor.

RP1 Patrick Bowen and I had returned from celebrating Eucharist at the first of two FOB's. We were twenty minutes delayed. Without this delay, our truck would have taken the hit rather than the truck which carried Marcous and Sean.

We tried to catch the chow run to Marcous' camp. Just before the chow hall, we saw the carnage on the side of the road. Blood was everywhere. Ambulances were arriving from the opposite direction. I knew the casualties, whoever they might be, would head to Bravo Surgical, so I scrambled out of the Humvee and ran there, still wearing my flak jacket and helmet. Then they arrived, Marcous and Sean. The trauma beds continued to fill. Over 35 casualties arrived from two other mortar attacks. One of the mortars hit just outside a tent of sleeping Marines.

Just two Sundays before, I had met Marcous at one of the FOB's for 3/1 Battalion. This FOB was very stark and had no running water and few amenities. I often led services in a tent with a flashlight and usually ministered to the Catholics only. However, Chaplain Ron Kennedy had been very sick, so I filled in for the non-denominational service. The faith of Marcous was alive and on fire. That night, Marcous shared that a corpsman had led him to Christ and that he was born again.

Love and faith blazed from Marcous' body as he lay wounded on the stretcher. This was no cursing, swearing or hardened Marine. This was a genuine disciple and soldier of Christ.

I walked from cot to cot and gurney to gurney looking into the faces and eyes of the injured. I felt as if I was just being. Being? What a ministry. It wasn't only the wounded who needed tending. Jesus must be allowed to overtake and permeate my being. The Body and the Blood I just ate catapult, motivate, and inebriate me. The precision of the words I speak or don't speak shocks me. I see eyes that are wild, confused, dazed. Nine of the casualties arrived just the day before. What a harsh welcome to the war zone.

Marcous asked for Chaplain Kennedy, his chaplain. I called 3-1 with no luck. He was probably on his way. I then prayed with Marcous; he made it so easy. During these moments, the medical team was in a flurry of activity, attending to the body while Marcous and I tended to his soul in an awesome state of peace. If faith can be visible, I saw it in Marcous. Nothing, absolutely nothing, was going to pierce his faith. Only two weeks prior,

Marcous and some of his fellow Marines had shared how they attributed their safety from an explosion to the deliverance of Jesus. They had felt shielded as the shrapnel from an IED had practically bounced off them.

By evening, Sean had lost a leg. The docs, nurses and staff frantically worked to save his other leg. Help us, Lord! Later, I finally managed to visit Sean and Marcous' FOB (camp). The truck's armor had been completely pierced. I understood how Sean's legs had been shattered. My stomach was queasy.

At the camp, I celebrated Mass with eleven Marines and sailors. I sought out the Battalion Commander who arrived late from Bravo Surgical. He usually attended Mass, and I thought he would certainly need Communion this night. Lt. Col. Willy Buhl regards his Marines and corpsmen as if they were his own sons. I felt honored to bring him the Bread of Life.

Upon returning to Bravo Surgical around 10-11:00 that night, I was exhausted. I quickly shed my forty pounds of flak jacket and helmet. Then I slipped in to visit Marcous. Sean had already been medevaced (flown out on a helicopter). Marcous would go soon. Only extreme medical cases were flown out without the cover of darkness.

His blanket was pulled off his chest. He was in the recovery room after emergency surgery. Marcous resembled images of Jesus in the upper room after the resurrection. He shared that his marriage had been troubled before his deployment to Iraq. His friend, the corpsman, brought him to Jesus. The corpsman's wife was now with his wife. He had been able to talk to her via satellite telephone. Marcous now prays with his wife. I can't imagine this young man before his conversion.

In the destruction of that Sunday when lives were changed in a ripple effect, I truly am grateful. My soul was rocked by God. Forever, I have moved closer to the Divine Compassionate One.

As I crawled into my bed with every ounce of energy depleted, I paused. I reflected. I rolled over and faced the cement wall next to my cot, and then it happened…

My Beloved touched me and whispered into my heart:

"I love you, Ron Moses. Thank you for being you, my beloved."

21 October 2004

GO REDSOX!

(It happened at 6:00 a.m., Iraq time!)

Jesus touches us in numerous ways, all ways and always. I grew up just outside Boston, Massachusetts. Baseball was a passion of mine but a sport I could not play. My eyes and lack of coordination wouldn't permit it. In fact, I was the only brother of six who did not play baseball or Little League. Yet today, after waiting and watching for years, the Red Sox dethroned the New York Yankees and are headed to the World Series. I spent four years living outside New York City from 1977-1981 when it was always the Damn Yankees. And here I am in an Iraqi combat zone, and the Red Sox seem poised to win the World Series for the first time since 1918. There have been precious few times the team ever even had the opportunity. The most recent occasion was in 1985 in which they lost to the NY Mets in the very last game.

So is this about prayer? Sure it is. I feel deliriously good. I am happy although I don't follow baseball too closely. I attended a game at Fenway Park earlier this year before deploying to Iraq. I love where I grew up and spent my childhood. I am so grateful for my parents. I was born about forty years **after** the last World Series Championship for the Red Sox. Sports are a diversion. They are supposed to be peaceful. Materialism, greed, and worship have spoiled much of the fun. Yet that is the struggle. Sports can be like the Wine of Life.

We all need wine. Jesus knew we needed a little bit of wine. It's our attempt to horde it that creates the problems. Don't worry, Jesus will make more…but first his mother will say, "Do whatever he tells you!"

Love one another.
Forgive one another.
Forgive the Yankees for winning time and time again.
Share with one another.
And praise God for our hands, feet, eyes and fun.
O, thank you Jesus for the Beloved and Hated …
Boston Red Sox!

For I, the Lord your God will hold your right hand, saying to you,
"Fear not, I will help you."

Isaiah 41:13

25 October 2004 — Too Young

I really don't know which I find more difficult for the heart: a person killed in action, an amputee, or a missing eye. For the dead, the story here is over. For the wounded, it is just beginning. Life goes on, but it will be a life remarkably transformed.

Unless someone puts God first in his or her life, then nothing will make much sense. True, this is my belief, but I know beyond a doubt that it is the truth. God loves all of us. God hears all of our prayers, even the whimpers, and must perform a triage of sorts. Yet fundamentally, God answers prayers in our favor, but the result is not for the world in which we live, but for the world prepared for God's beloved ones, that is, all of us.

Jesus said, "Whoever is not with me is against me." I believe him.

I lift up PFC Brian Oliviera who died from an explosion playing football with a group of Marines and sailors. Various forms of shrapnel lodged in the wounded bodies of fifteen men. Shrapnel strikes at the soul. It is killing me. Most of the injured are lance corporals and privates and third class corpsmen. They are almost always very young, around 19-24 years of age. Brian has a one-month-old son, which means he will never see his child. The son will never know his father.

War stinks.

From my sketchy notes:

+ PFC Brian Oliviera – *Anointing and Last Rites just before he died in the trauma room. Hoang Thai, the corpsman, did a great job to keep him alive. I spoke with Hoang, and his wounds are in his heart and soul.*

Nicholas Fox – *Catholic, Anointed*

Sgt Grant Belvin – *Baptist*

Justin Garcia – *Pentecostal, He asked me to teach him how to pray a Rosary given to him*

Cpl West – *neck injury*

Jason Roldan – *Catholic, Anointing/*

Steven McCurran –*Catholic, Anointing*

Greg Smith – *Catholic, Anointing*

John Robertson – *Non-Denominational*

PFC Chavez, Edward – *neck*

PFC McLaughlin, Matthew –

CPL Perea, Timothy – *(can't read my notes)*

Jason Gome – *Christian*

Germain Ung – *Buddhist, eye. As I talked to him, I encouraged him to breathe like the Buddhists. He couldn't see me but recognized my voice. "Father Ron, I had dinner with you last night when you were at our camp." I remembered immediately. We laughed even though his situation was grave. I had met many of these men before, and this was getting difficult. I located a religious Buddhist gift given to Germain by his father which had been removed. I placed it around his neck. We prayed peacefully* *and bridged our faiths. The surgeon and the doctor expected Germain to lose his eye and he was a sharpshooter. However, we learned two weeks later that Germain miraculously regained his full sight. Let us rejoice!*

Matthew Baxter – *Catholic, Anointing*

Edward Wright – *Catholic, Anointing (arm)*

30 & 31 October 2004

My Soul is Burnt & Crushed

The eve of All Saints:

Amidst hatred and barren ground, my heart, blood and soul are burnt, crushed, and forgotten.

O Beloved, is there any other way?

This whole scene is ghoulish. Before the push for Fallujah, already the carnage is rotten.

Eight Marines were burned. Nine Marines and sailors were wounded. Countless others are dealing with the reality of war. There are more fatherless children in the world. There are now more widows. There are more parents wailing.

Last night, the shrapnel injuries were not as devastating in the wounded, but many souls were burnt and tortured. How does one fathom the toll?

For the Lord does not see as humans do. Humans look at outward appearances, but the Lord looks at the heart.

I am drained but not broken. The tragedy and immensity of war are well beyond my grasp. It seems inappropriate to share this at any time, but maybe some day. Maybe?

Amazing Grace, how sweet the sound…

That saved and set me free.

I once was lost, but now am found.

Was blind but now I see.

The Prophet speaks:

God will destroy death forever;

The Lord will wipe away the tears from all faces;

The reproach of his people he will remove from the whole earth;

For the Lord has spoken.

Isaiah 28:8

O God, hear my prayer - to you all flesh must come.

+ **Jonathan Byrd** *(expecting child January 12th)*

+ **Michael Scarborough**

+ **Sgt Courtney, Kelly**

+ **John Lukac** *(Met his parents when I returned stateside)*

+**Travis Fox** *(married)*

+**Andrew Rydel**

+ **Jeremy Bowen**

+ **Chris Lapka**

+ **Slokum?** *(Sometimes I couldn't decipher names.)*

Chapter VII

NOVEMBER IN FALLUJAH

(The Battle for Fallujah)

Muslim Tears

2 November 2004 **Feast of All Souls**

A Baptist man was referred to me. His wife, the mother of his children, had been unfaithful. He was wounded and bleeding profusely in his heart and soul.

I have often received this kind of moral casualty. There is no morphine to dull or numb the pain. No anesthesia exists for the spiritual surgery I must perform. The man's only chance for a life is the opposite of what feels right or justified. He must forgive his wife. Yes.

He must then allow himself to be forgiven. This is not easy. In fact, it seems nearly impossible. Maybe this is why God came to Earth, suffered and died. God loves us so much, and God understands our fears…

God came to show us the Way. God knows. God cares. God loves.

Only Yahweh, Jesus, the Son of God, was the sole divine being who lived among us, suffered, and died for us. God did this not to make us feel guilty and blindly worship him. God calls us to be friends and not slaves.

We are beloved of God.
Let us love one another as God loves us.

Oh, give thanks to the Lord, for he is good! For his mercy endures forever.
1 Chronicles 16:34

Annoyed about some petty thing, I was summoned to assist one dead and five wounded Iraqi soldiers. What I witnessed, however, was not a soldier at all but a human being killed by hateful enemies of peace and God.

Before my eyes, the bloody and dead man lay in the back of a pick-up truck. He was the father of nine. As his broken body was removed from the truck, a fellow soldier sat beside him. They had been close friends. The man sobbed, cried out in anguish, and screamed, as he tried to understand what appeared to be senseless. That moment, in front of the hospital, he realized his friend could not be fixed, for we brought him not into the hospital, but to Mortuary Affairs.

I needed to embrace him, and I didn't.

It wasn't in him.

It wasn't in me.

The translator showed me,

but I failed to respond at first.

Forgive me, my friend.

Then Chief Damon Sanders, whom I was preparing for the Sacraments, caught this man and I held him, too. I couldn't speak the language. The soldier was inconsolable. My heart was angry; my tears were hot.

What kinds of animals do this? What does the enemy want? More hatred?

Muhammad doesn't care for this. How come he can't help us now? How does Allah sit back and do nothing? No words of comfort, only praise of Allah. In a strange way, my praising of Allah calmed this friend, this man. Using the translator, I asked the man to look into my eyes. I allowed him to see my eyes and look through the window of my soul. And we bridged the gap between cultures, religions, and languages. I could not remove his pain or sorrow. This was not the time. The few surreal minutes seemed suspended in a place that was neither heaven nor hell. In a sense, the experience was darn right terrifying. And yet it was peaceful. Forever I will remember his burning tears rubbing against my hands and heart. One day, all brothers will be united in a bond of love. A day that must hurry, for I cannot bear this much longer.

Jesus, you taught us not to praise the Father with lip service. You taught us to love one another.

Jesus, you are still with us. Your body left, but your Spirit remains.

Be with us, Lord, be with us!

RP1 Patrick Bowen, USNR - Abu Ghraib Prison

When we listen to your word, our minds are filled with light.

-It is the lowly heart that understands.

From the Office of Readings

Maccabees 3:1-26

They said to Judas, "How can we, few as we are, fight such a mighty host as this? Besides, we are weak today from fasting." But Judas said, "It is easy for many to be overcome by a few. In the sight of Heaven there is no difference between deliverance by many or by a few; for victory in war does not depend upon the size of the army, but on strength that comes from Heaven."

" With great presumption and lawlessness they come against us to destroy us and our wives and children and to despoil us; but we are fighting for our lives and our laws. He himself will crush them before us; so do not be afraid of them."

Guadium et Spes: *(Vatican II Document)*

We must all undergo a change of heart. We must look out on the whole world and see the tasks that we can all do together to promote the well-being of the family of man. We must not be misled by a false sense of hope.

Unless antagonism and hatred are abandoned, unless binding and honest agreements are concluded, safeguarding universal peace in the future, mankind, already in grave peril, may well face in spite of its marvelous advance in knowledge that day of disaster when it knows no other peace than the awful peace of death.

To build peace, the causes of human discord which feed the fires of war must first be eliminated, and among these especially the violations of justice. Many of these causes are due to gross economic inequality and delay in providing necessary remedies. Others arise from a spirit of domination and from contempt for others, and, among more fundamental causes, from human envy, distrust, pride and other forms of selfishness. Since man cannot bear so many violations of due order, the result is that, even where war does not rage, the world is constantly plagued by human conflict and acts of violence.

Christians, especially young Christians, deserve praise and support when they offer themselves voluntarily in the service of other people and other nations. Indeed, it is the duty of all God's people, with bishops giving a lead by word and example, to do all in their power to relieve the sufferings of our times, following the age-old custom of the Church in giving not only what they can spare but also what they need for themselves.

Naked I came forth from my mother's womb,
and naked I shall go back again.
The Lord gave and the Lord has taken away;
blessed be the name of the Lord!
We accept good things from God;
and should we not accept evil?
Job 1:21, 2:10

4 November 2004 **Thursday**

God is our refuge and strength, a very present help in trouble.

\- Psalm 46:1

Still Hanging On

5 November 2004 **Friday Afternoon**

Four Army troops came into Bravo Surgical. One clung to life as the others dealt with their injuries. I wrote the following notes in my green journal:

+ Camacho-Rivera, Carlos – *Catholic – He died after leaving Bravo Surgical (Anointing, Apostolic Blessing, Forgiveness) Still hanging on – God help us. Intercession of St. Charles Boremeo*
Green, Kellee – *abdomen, Christian (Prayer) Army*
Robinson, Rodrick SPC – *Jesus/Cross (prayer) Army*
Lopez, Richard – *Christian (prayer)*

The exact events are hard to remember. It was around 1400 (2:00 p.m.) on a beautiful day. I anointed Carlos Camacho-Rivera and gave him the Apostolic Blessing, which pardons all sins. It is an occasion similar to when Jesus hung on the cross between two thieves. One of the thieves cried out to Jesus after admonishing his brother thief, "Jesus, remember me when you come into your kingdom." Even as Jesus suffered tremendously, he turned to the thief and said, "Today you will be with me in Paradise." Now if God promises, it is a done deal.

In my weakness, however, I wanted Carlos to live. I desperately wanted people to witness miraculous healings from my priesthood. Of course, I didn't want anyone to know this dark side of me. I had forgiven Carlos all of his sins. He was pure and ready to go to heaven. He had been in the battle with his brother Marines, probably cursing or not fully living up to his Baptismal promises. None of us do. We are all just pilgrims passing through this world. I believe God wired us to be lonely. Carlos' purpose in life was to be called to Our Creator, but I, Ron, didn't want that. I was struggling big time.

I had experienced approximately twenty deaths. I was very restless. This was different. I wanted more than anything for this young man to live. My heart was about to explode. I wanted to run away, but there was nowhere to go.

St. Augustine (354-430 A.D.) was directed in life by philosophy, hedonism and perverse things. He most often quoted in his *Confessions,* "You have made us for yourself, and our heart is restless until it rests in you." Not unlike many of our young troops, Augustine lived with a woman with whom he was not married. He fathered a son outside of marriage. His life centered on himself. When these very young men and women in Iraq come into the realm of my ministry, I don't judge them. I accept them as they are, knowing they will all eventually give into this God of Love. They seem so lonely and needy, yet their feelings are the last things they desire to reveal to anyone, especially themselves.

"We see therefore that, for St. Augustine, loneliness is both a good and a natural thing. It is God's way of drawing us toward the life for which we were made. God wants us to live inside the divine life, and so God placed within us a strong erotic thirst, a loneliness, that forces us to constantly yearn for God and to be frustrated and not content when we are outside of God's life." (Ronald Rolheiser, The Restless Heart, p 112, Doubleday, 2004)

The philosopher, Blaise Pascal, once remarked, "The sole cause of man's unhappiness is that he does not know how to stay quietly in his room." How true! Yet how natural! For Augustine, this is not a great mystery or an astounding anomaly. We cannot stay quietly in our rooms precisely because God did not build us to stay quietly in a room. We were built to wander, to be restless and lonely. Accordingly, we should not be surprised if we find ourselves incurably in that condition. (Ibid.) These are precisely the kinds of people who come into the desert of Iraq. We are all lonely.

Strangely enough, the medieval theologian, Thomas Aquinas, added a dimension that could be the solution to the great divide between East and West, North and South. Loneliness is not just a thirst for God but a thirst for other persons and the world as well. According to Aquinas, complete rest for our lonely hearts will come only when we are in full union with God, with each other, and with all of reality. Thus, Aquinas would recast slightly the Augustinian dictum, making it read: You have made us for yourself, and our heart is restless until it rests in you...*and others, and the whole world.* (Rolheiser, pp 113, 114)

So, still waiting for a miracle, I walked outside to the front of the hospital. I prayed for an intercession of St. Charles Boremeo, the saint of the day. Then I started praying the Rosary. My heart felt heavy. I must have looked at least 100 years old. Is this what it would feel like to experience the death of one's own flesh and blood?

I just couldn't finish the Rosary. I was sitting on the steps to a platform used to drag dead bodies from tanks. I was numb and stunned. A young marine sergeant asked if he could help me. With heavy eyes, I nodded my head with the rosary wilted in my hands. The Marine was Catholic, yet he had been struggling to return to the Sacraments and the Life of the Church. We had talked on another occasion in which I had been the strong one, the fatherly figure. Today, he was also like a son to me, just like Carlos who was in the process of dying. Mark sat beside me on the steps, and we prayed the Rosary together. The end of each Hail Mary felt like a dagger to my heart and an assurance to me. "Holy Mary, Mother of God, pray for us sinners now **and at the hour of our death.** Amen."

We watched the helicopter evacuate Carlos. I knew he would die. Not only was Carlos holding on to his life on Earth, but I was holding on, too! Every injury was partly my injury. Every death was part of my death.

How much could I take? The answer was fast approaching.

+ Carlos M. Camacho-Rivera

In April of 2008, I found the following excerpt of an article from The Atlanta Journal-Constitution:

Army Sgt. Carlos M. Camacho-Rivera (ajc.com/news)

Carlos M. Camacho-Rivera was the guy you wanted in your convoy. During one mission, he was flagged down after a fuel tanker accidentally rammed a Humvee, pinning two soldiers inside.

"The scene was horrific, everyone was in a state of shock," recalled Capt. Erik Hilberg. But Camacho took charge, working with others to rig a wrecker truck with chains and lift the tanker off the truck.

"He worked with speed and precision," Hilberg said. "He had nerves of steel."

Both soldiers were freed, recovered from their injuries and returned to duty.

"We all agree, no one else on the road could have done it," Hilberg said.

Camacho-Rivera, 24, of Carolina, Puerto Rico, died Nov. 5 in a rocket attack in Fallujah. He was based at Fort Story.

He is survived by his wife, Tania, and son, Carlos Jr., 3.

Camacho-Rivera left two letters to be opened in the event of his death. One was to his wife, the other to a fellow soldier, who shared parts of it at the memorial service.

"He said he knew he would be fine, and he knew now he would be someone's guardian angel," Hilberg said.

6 & 7 November 2004: Weekend before Al Fajr

The days and weeks rushed together. Every day since our arrival on September 6, there have been casualties. Even on the day we had a mass casualty drill, the wounded came as we were evaluating our preparation. On Saturdays and Sundays, I have been celebrating Mass and hearing confessions. I began teaching adult formation classes on Sundays and Tuesdays. Some of the Marines and sailors are assisting me in preparing over twenty-four people for the Sacraments of Initiation into the Catholic Church (RCIA). Sometimes, I catch troops in the field or on the run. Watches and duties often prevent them from attending the formal classes. RP1 Patrick Bowen has been great with his computer skills in preparing Masses and classes. We were able to view holy pictures on a big screen and have music at our services.

At Camp Fallujah, approximately 150 to 300 people attended Mass every weekend. Patrick and I also ventured out to at least five other locations for Mass. Sometimes, twenty-five of us would cram into a small space, but other times only three or four would attend. Each time I celebrated Mass, I entered into this central prayer of my life as if it were my first Mass, my only Mass and my last Mass. This served me well. I could begin Mass absolutely drained physically, mentally, emotionally and spiritually, but feel rejuvenated afterwards.

There was no time to feel sorry for myself or to wish I was somewhere else because we were so busy. I actively visited and ministered to many patients, conversed with the staff, and prepared homilies. I was frequently in active prayer. Often, I prayed the Rosary during the convoys to different locations. Fear often took over for a short moment but then transformed into peace. I really wasn't very afraid. I simply felt protected and guarded. Maybe all the prayers from people at home suspended me.

My duties included spiritual counseling. Sometimes, I used my counseling background. There are so many hurting and isolated people among us. In the desert, I found the troops more open to the spiritual world within themselves. They greatly hungered to be in harmony with life. Yet, I believe there will never be harmony within any of us until we die. The world must be some kind of great school in which we never finish our studies. At St. Patrick's parish, we called it "ongoing conversion."

This particular weekend, I celebrated Mass for the Army and a group of Marines. Some would die in a few days or weeks. Some would experience a battle that would stain their lives forever. They would all know someone who died or who experienced debilitating wounds. Giving them Communion provided me with a whole new perspective.

Battle for Fallujah

7 November 2004 **Phantom Fury- Vigil**

Here I am, somehow caught up in this battle in the desert. Our President believes it is specifically to conquer terrorism and the evil forces of the enemy. He truly believes God is on his side. I don't think terrorism will ever be conquered. It is like trying to eliminate hatred. Brothers have been hating brothers since the beginning of the human race. It is part of us. God help us.

10,000 troops from the United States of America are staged here in Fallujah. We say this is a coalition force. I see American troops, some Iraqi troops but hardly any troops from other countries.

I am the Catholic priest at Bravo Surgical. I am the only Catholic priest here. The injured and the "Angels," or the dead, funnel through here.

Surgeons, doctors, nurses, corpsmen and Marines are staged and ready. Bravo Surgical has a motto: "Cheaters of Death." We are moving to say instead, "Ready to Receive." We have already experienced quite a few casualties.

This whole thing is bloody and confusing. If an enemy insurgent arrives whose injuries are slightly worse than an American's…we must treat the insurgent first. O how I want to go home, yet I am dragged into this mess. I want to run away like Jonah. I know God will prevail. I know God is planning something beautiful. I don't fear death.

St. Ambrose: *Office of Readings*

"Death" in this context is a Passover to be made by all mankind. You must keep facing it with perseverance. It is a Passover from corruption, from mortality to immortality, from rough seas to a calm harbor. The word "death' must not trouble us; the blessings that come from a safe journey should bring us joy. What is death but the burial of sin and the resurrection of goodness? Scripture says: "*Let my soul die among the souls of the just*," so that I may cast off my sins and put on the grace of the just, of those who bear the death of Christ with them, in their bodies and in their souls.

Saint Paul to Timothy in his second letter (2:11-12):

> *Here is a saying you can depend on: If we have died with him, we shall also live with him; if we suffer with him, we shall also reign with him.*

God was preparing me for what was to come.

10 & 11 November — Phantom Fury: Al Fajr

Two Marines were in serious trouble. I had planned to go to bed but decided to hang around. I am almost deliriously tired. In fact, I may be too tired to cry. Even my tears feel dry and lonely. Gene and Joseph were in Trauma Beds One and Two. At first, there were too many people in the room. And then I saw their dog tags, both of which said, 'Roman Catholic.' I love the Church, especially the notion that at the moment of death, we can shout, "I am Catholic! I want my Father!" How can I be Father? I've not raised these boys, yet at the moment of need, they beg for strength, courage and the life of Our Father; "You O Lord! Father, Dad, Beloved!"

"I can't do it!" I shout to God in the core of my being.

"You can do it!" God shouts back to me.

O no Jesus! They must let go of everything! I believe, I believe, I believe! But they don't always believe. It seems they must be taught in the fleeting moments woven with terror and fear…your love. Their last contact with this wretched world needs to be love.

Gene's friends were hovering as the docs and nurses searched for fragments of his life. However, I didn't know they were his friends. I didn't know this Marine was a member of Bravo Surgical just a few months ago. How would I know this? I moved away from Gene when I read his eyes…his body would no longer hold onto his soul. The tattooed dragon on his right shoulder would remain until his skin was no more, but Gene was moving forward. God promised. God is faithful. Today you will be with me in paradise.

Gene passed out after I anointed him, and I moved to Joseph in Trauma Bed Two. Joseph was the son of Monica. I encouraged Joseph to breathe in and out. Joseph was getting cold, and I stood near his head. It seemed my place was reserved, yet I didn't understand. O Jesus, I didn't know what to do. Somehow, I felt so inadequate, like I didn't know what I was doing. The stones covering our hearts are so terrifyingly big.

The most important matters in my life at this moment were saying the Jesus prayer and teaching Joseph to breathe. Here I was, coaching again. I rubbed Joseph's head, held his hand, searched for ways to warm him, and encouraged him with whispers. He was so thirsty, and I couldn't give him anything. I desperately wanted to give him a drink, but he was going into surgery. I felt ill-prepared for this. I felt I hadn't fasted or sacrificed enough for my prayers to be answered. The doctors cut Gene's side to massage his heart. He couldn't breathe, so I returned to him. My words were jumbled…they are for the living…I knew Gene would die…yet I said nothing…I couldn't…Help me to understand!!!!!

Joseph was then moved into the operating room…and I carried things that needed to be moved, and I found myself in the room. I talked to Joseph all the way but not before seeing the doctors were letting Gene go.

I left the operating room and returned to the trauma room as Gene's face was being covered. I rushed into the room silently saying, "No!" I held his head in my hands that break the sacred bread of the Body and Blood of Jesus…and I prayed; I don't know what…

I prayed the prayer attached to Gene's dog tags that also stated he was Roman Catholic:

Dear Lord Jesus,

I realize I am a sinner.

I repent for my sins and right this moment

I receive you as my Lord and Savior. Amen.

I will be strong and courageous.

I will not be terrified, or discouraged for the Lord is with me

Wherever I go!

I bent down and kissed Gene's forehead. I truly loved him even though I had just met him. Later, with Mortuary Affairs Marines and with his friends, I prayed and then sang.

Into your hands O Lord,
we commend the Body and Soul of
+ Gene Ramirez.
If God is for us, who can be against us?
Give us rest O Lord!

* *Joseph Heredia died in Germany ten days later, on November 20. I didn't hear the news until over a year later as I was writing this book at Prince of Peace Monastery in Oceanside, California. I really loved this kid and expected him to make it. My heart breaks for his poor mother, Monica. Please lift her up in prayer.*

Chaplains and RP's gathered on Yom Kippur. I am in the back row, farthest right. The chaplain's office is behind the wall on the left.

Just after celebrating Mass in Fallujah. Notice the altar that Patrick Bowen set and fashioned with MRE boxes. These men are from 3-5 Marines.

In the City of Fallujah and I call it "Jailed in Iraq." Even though I was on the outside, I felt imprisoned in my soul.

Another brother chaplain flanked by an Army and a Navy "body guard": Chaplain Protectors!

Chaplain Dwight Horn (Presbyterian Chaplain) stood beside me before going to the men in the City of Fallujah. Dwight became a great friend and was an incredible asset to Marine Battalion 3-5.

LT Colonel Buhl, SGT Major, Padre and friend
Abu Ghraib Prison with Lima Company
(5 October 2004)

The Death of Saint Martin de Tours

11 November 2004 10:35 in the morning

Life is a gift.

Enjoy.

When our life runs its course we can only imagine

what will be next.

For love created us into being.

And love carries us forever into being.

Just imagine!

In a letter written by Sulpicius Severus on the death of Saint Martin de Tours:

Thereupon he broke into tears, for he was a man in whom the compassion of our Lord was continually revealed. Turning to our Lord, he made this reply to their pleading: "Lord if your people still need me, I am ready for the task; your will be done."

Here was a man words cannot describe. Death could not defeat him nor toil dismay him. He was quite without preference of his own; he neither feared to die nor refused to live. With eyes and hands always raised to heaven he never withdrew his unconquered spirit from prayer...

... "Allow me, brothers, to look toward heaven rather than at the earth, so that my spirit may set on the right course when the time comes for me to go on my journey to the Lord."

As he spoke these words, he saw the devil standing near. "Why do you stand there, you blood thirsty brute?" he cried. "Murderer, you will not have me for your prey. Abraham is welcoming me into his embrace."

With these words, he gave his spirit to heaven. Filled with joy, Martin was welcomed by Abraham. Thus he left this life a poor and lowly man and entered heaven rich in God's favor.

It was twelve days since my last journal entry. There was no break in the flow of casualties to Bravo Surgical.

+ **Theodore Holder, SSGT**

+ Kyle Burns, LCPL

(Same day Matthew Brown and his St. Michael Medal came in)

Theodore and Kyle were pronounced dead in the parking lot of Bravo Surgical as their bloody bodies were removed from their LAR tanks. It was one of the most gruesome sights of my life. I didn't expect blood to coagulate in that way. I ministered to the young Marines who had been in the vehicles with these gunners.

They were in desperate need of ministry. One of them was in total shock.

I anointed three of these men because I believed their experience was debilitating psychologically, emotionally and spiritually.

+ Nathan Anderson

One solitary tear

12 November 2004 **Camp Fallujah**

Awoken for another 'angel'

Baptist, Jonathan.

I hadn't showered in about four days. The smell of death was beginning to cling to my uniform. Mortuary Affairs didn't have a chaplain at the time, and since I was attached to Bravo Surgical just a few feet away, I was the closest minister. I wanted to be present for the soldiers, Marines and sailors who were brought in dead. I wanted to offer a prayer, a song, or a cry to God for help. But I was tired and not used to this constant flow of casualties day and night. I felt like I was in a marathon race and hitting the wall.

The Battle for Fallujah was just beginning. I had already prayed with the bodies of about twenty-nine men and woman who had died. There had been hundreds of casualties. All I wanted to do was shower and blow some of the death out of my nostrils. I packed my backpack and shower gear and stumbled to Mortuary Affairs with arthritis and self-pity nipping at my ankles and feet.

I walked into the room and there he was, Jonathan, who had life and breath in him just a short time ago. He was young, ruddy and handsome. But he was dead. His dog tags said his faith was Baptist. I breathed in, as I coach all of the casualty patients to do, and I recoiled at the smell of death. I prayed by singing "Amazing Grace" and placed my hand upon his head. I hoped he would breathe again, but my faith was not that strong. I left for the shower about one hundred yards away in a row of trailers. I was clueless as to what the Lord had planned for me.

As I stood at the sink ready to lather shaving cream on my face, the commanding officer of Bravo Surgical informed me there was another casualty in Trauma Bed Two who was dying. I wanted to take a shower. I felt like going to bed. I continued to shave, even a bit defiantly, though I knew I should return to the hospital. Yet, if I hadn't taken those few extra minutes to shear the stubble from my face, I might have missed the rest of this story. God knew better than me. I trudged back to the clinic. My delay caused me to be caught in the narrow hallway between the trauma and operating rooms.

I was forced into the operating room. The soldier on the stretcher looked awful. His name was Edward, and his red hair was cut tight to his head. Catching sight of me, the surgeon and nurses began giving me orders. A female doc or nurse shouted at me, "He's Catholic!"

Something was happening.

I saw it all - blood, his body cut open, his exposed heart pumping.

An eleven-inch cylindrical piece of metal was pulled out of his abdomen.

How in the world had he survived? How had he lived this long?

I held a plasma bag as instructed, squeezing it out. I had never been in a functioning operating room before. The doctors told me to help lift and pull Edward onto the table. What else would I be asked to do? I dredged my mind, searching for a prayer or the right words; I was anxious, yet peaceful. How long could I do this? What was I doing here?

I stood in the corner of the cramped room with all the machines and tubes and blood and stayed out of the way, trying to catch my breath. I was startled as the surgeon barked out, "Set up the light!" I would have ignored him except I was standing on it. So I followed his orders. As I wrestled with the huge, metal light, I felt as if I was throwing out prayers hoping to get a basket.

Eventually, it was just my spirit with Edward. There was no hope, no medical hope. Finally, I could talk with Edward. He was dying. I told him so.

I caressed his head and red hair, shared the Word in the midst of all of the blood and bodily fluid and chaos. And then as I sang *'O Holy Night;'* a song of birth, **a single solitary tear** slipped down his face.

O weary world, how can we rejoice? When will we rejoice again?

Jesus, o beloved, you wept with Mary and Martha.

Edward was there; Edward was here, saving this single tear… For me?

For his family?

For the world?

For you?

Jesus wept when he knew but was present for his beloved people.

Was it you, Jesus, in the middle of all this mess?

Fall on my knees

I hear the Angel's voice calling

O night divine

Throughout the night birth

Don't be afraid; for behold, I proclaim to you good news of great joy that will be for all people. Behold, I am with you always, until the end of time.

I said more prayers and anointed Edward with holy oils.

Time was running out for Edward, and I needed to say something, but it was hard for me. I wanted to say I loved him, but that isn't easy for guys to do, even priests sometimes.

And then this force came from within me, from a depth I didn't know I had. It formed my heart, my compassion and my thoughts into words:

"I love you, Edward"

A flash of light

A kiss on his forehead

And life as we know it left him.

"Go with God, Beloved Edward. Go with God."

Amen

Eucharist.

12 November 2004

+ Jonathan Shields (*watched soul depart)*

+ Edward Iwan *(a single tear)*

+ James Patrick Blecksmith

+ James Matteson

+ Douglas ?

+ David ?

13 November 2004

+ Jose Valez

+Joseph Urban Seiford

+Donald Renthusen

+Sean Simms

+Byron Norwood

+ Justin M. Ellsworth

+Kevin Dempsey

+ Justin McLeese

+ Benjamin Bryan

+ Victor Ronald Lu

14 November 2004

+George Payton

+ Dale Burger

+ Nicholas Ziokowski

+ (Three whose names are not clear)

George

14 November 2004

At 8:30 a.m., the Sacrifice of the Mass began. I broke the body of my Lord, at his command. I watched the blood pour out of his body into the cup to be shared with his friends. For those who could not receive, I traced the cross with the blood on my thumb onto their foreheads. It was messy.

After the Eucharist, with Jesus in me, I returned to my room, casting off my armored vest and helmet. Then I was notified a man was in the operating room. He had already lost a leg; a grenade had exploded beneath him.

I did not know his religious faith before entering the room. In Iraq, there were Muslims, Jews, Atheists, Agnostics, Catholics, Lutherans, Episcopalians, other Protestants, Buddhists, or whatever.

As chaplain, I searched for a connection in this worldly world. I know the truth. I am getting to know God. I love God who loves me more. God is all compassionate beyond our wildest dreams. God respects all human beings despite our sinfulness and brokenness. It is clear that Satan, the Evil One, was at large in Iraq. This was not in any way a reflection of the Iraqi people; they, too, were suffering. Rather, the hideous, disgusting and cowardly image of evil we call Satan was revealed in the ravages and tumult of war.

And so, as I trudged the past days through the wounded, bludgeoned and destroyed flesh, it was Jesus among us and within me who entered into this very dark, sad and fiery hell. I had no fear with my Friend, my Beloved beside me. Jesus

I AM

When I approached the operating room door, I noticed blood tracked in the hallway. It was sticky. The smell of blood and impending death once more began to flood my nostrils and spirit. The team, the wonderful team of docs, nurses and corpsmen, were frustrated with the carnage on the table. What I saw, what I took in, was the Lamb of God, being slaughtered.

One leg was gone. Blood was like a pool around the table leading to the door where I stood. My mental image of Abraham almost killing his son has now been colored in bright scarlet red.

As I swam to the table through the blood, George's hands and arms were outstretched in a cruciform. Blood seeped from every hole and orifice of his body, including those manmade ones, with the exception of his eyes and nose.

In his right hand were his dog tags. Religious preference is listed at the bottom. So I searched and read, "Christian." There was no other evidence of this man's faith. His tattoos were almost contrary to the term, 'Christian.' Yet, this was my opening. Jesus was opening the door for me to enter into the Gift. "Today you will be with me in Paradise."

I tiptoed, trying to avoid getting George's blood on my uniform or shoes. It was impossible. By this time, it wasn't even George's blood anymore … for he had received the gift of others' blood a number of times.

And so, I prayed with George. I placed my hand upon his head, gently, and whispered words of love and encouragement. I forgave his sins as my Master commanded me to do. I sang as blood and fluids could not stay within him and would not clot. The Christ, the slaughtered Lamb of God, kept pouring out blood.

Then again, just like a couple days earlier with Edward who had died before me, a single tear rolled only halfway down George's face before it froze.

Water and blood. Only those close to the crucifixion of our Lord saw it. Water and Blood.

George did not die on that table yesterday, or did he? Did he die to the world, as he knew it before this day? I hope and pray that he did.

O compassionate and merciful Jesus, I know you hear our prayers. If we ask, you give if it is for our good and not evil.

Give George Life.

Thank you.

I whispered to George, "I love you."

Again, as I did earlier this week with another man, I kissed him on the forehead.

He is in your hands, Beloved Jesus.

He is in your hands.

God, You are so good…All the Time.

+ George Payton, 20 (3rd Battalion 5th Marines)

During high school, George J. Payton's mother sent him to live with relatives in Fiji because she worried about the influence of gangs in their Los Angeles neighborhood. A year later, he returned focused and mature, and he joined the Marines in 2002. "He was getting around to becoming the kind of man I wanted him to be," said his mother, Chandra, a literacy coach. "He was my confidante, my support, my right hand." Payton, 20, of Culver City, Calif., died in a hostile attack on Nov. 14. He was stationed at Camp Pendleton, Calif. Payton was near the end of his second tour in Iraq and in one of his last letters home, he told his mother not to send any more care packages. "He wrote that he had a strange feeling that something would happen to him, that he'd probably come home before December," his mother said. "I thought maybe so, but I thought he'd come home alive." (The Washington Post)

15 November 2004

+ Rafael Peralta

+ Bradly Parker

+ Travis Desiato

+ James Swain

+ S. E. Kielion

+ Gene Ramirez + Joseph Heredia + Jonathan Shields

+ Edward D. Iwan + Dale A. Burger, Jr. + Travis Desiato

+ Jessica Cawvey + Nazario Serrano + In C. Kim

I am in the "B" of this aerial view of Bravo Surgical.

After the Battle for Fallujah with a Yankee fan.

ANGELIC BIRTH

The following day, after Dale (Chapter I) passed over to the other side, I sat down for dinner at the chow hall. It was lamb. I had thought that lamb would be less processed than most of the other meat we ate, so I gave thanks and savored the first bite of it in my mouth.

Suddenly, I felt a tap on my shoulder. RP1 Patrick Bowen stood beside me and informed me there was another "expectant angel" on the ward. He was Roman Catholic.

I stood immediately and wrapped my dinner. Patrick had already arranged the ambulance. It would transport me the short distance to the Marine with a gunshot sniper wound to the head. He was almost in the exact condition as Dale had been, except his breathing was being helped by a faithful corpsman.

We didn't know his first name except that his initials were S.E.

Immediately, I noticed two guardian angels tattooed on S.E.'s chest. I also noticed a tattooed Bible with praying hands under his right arm on the side of his chest. Quite evidently under his left arm was a tattoo of his dog tag:

S. E. Kielion

012 34 777

CATHOLIC

This time Gunny had moved closer. He was holding S.E.'s hand with tears streaming down his face. I encouraged him with a hand on his shoulder and met his eyes. I prayed. We all prayed. Heaven prayed. Then the Church anointed him. I desperately wanted to use his first name, but it was not available at that moment. Was it Stephen? Did he speak as Saint Stephen just before his death by stoning, "Father forgive them, they know not what they do."

In the depths of my heart, I knew S. E. Kielion asked Jesus to send me to his side in his last few breaths in this weary and war-torn world. I was in awe again- privileged, honored, humbled, and speechless. Prayers and love flowed out of me like a spring of life giving water. God used me like an instrument of peace.

This beautiful and holy man died all too quickly after I arrived. I desperately wanted to spend time with him like Martha and Mary felt about their brother, Lazarus. Everyone thought Jesus had arrived too late to heal Lazarus, his beloved friend. Jesus wept after Mary, surrounded by her friends, fell at his feet with her grief and cried out, "Lord, if you had been here, my brother would not have died." Some said, "See how he loved him." But then some of them said, "Could not the one who opened the eyes of the blind man have done something so that this man would not have died?"

The details are fuzzy, but fading images have surfaced. I dipped my thumb in holy oils and traced the cross on S.E.'s bloody forehead. I placed my hand on his chest over the tattooed angels, and my heart was flooded with coursing tears that never reached my eyes. I looked into the eyes of those around me.

An agnostic doctor, Brian, pronounced the Marine dead. The doctor was a friendly and mild-mannered man who struggled with faith like we all do. His eyes were swimming in tears. O there are so many words spoken with the eyes, and sometimes they contradict each other. I suppose I had run out of tears and searched the eyes of others for that elixir of the body. On the cross, just before he died an agonizing and fluid-draining ordeal, Jesus cried out, "**I thirst!**" Incredibly, our tears could quench his thirst.

I listen lately to the sound of a tear rumbling, babbling, streaking down a face of love and grief and fear. I'm not sure the sound of a tear is heard with ears that have been barraged with rockets, mortars, amplified music and city sounds.

In Haiti, amidst the oppressive and relentless poverty and desperation, the people have a proverb: *If a mosquito piddles in the ocean, the water rises.*

I suppose, I trust, that if a tear of love is shed for a sinner, even if the sinner happens to be me, God notices, and the angels rejoice. And we will all arise again with Jesus, with Lazarus and with S. E. Kielion.*

S.E. Kielion

A couple of months later, I learned that S. E. Kielion was only 23 and had married his high school sweetheart, April. His wife gave birth to their first and only son at exactly the same time of his death. The child's name is* ***S. E. Kielion, JR.* *At the funeral, nearly the whole city of Omaha, Nebraska came out, including the Mayor. April and* ***Shane*** *were very faithful Catholics and had attended Catholic schools. Their elementary school, St. Bernadette, held a baby shower for the family. I met April in a hotel lobby in Omaha about twenty-nine months after Shane's death.*

16 November 2004

17 November 2004

18 November 2004

+ Joseph Nolan

19 November 2004

+ Gavriel Demetrius

+ Dennis Brown, SSGT

+ Luis Figuroa

Five Masses in the City of Fallujah

21 November 2004

In the last two weeks I personally cared for about forty angels (KIA) at Bravo Surgical. On this day, I would travel into the devastation in the center of Fallujah. Men to whom I had ministered in the camps had experienced hell and desperately needed a chaplain. The Battle for Fallujah was essentially over, but I would still receive another twenty deaths along with hundreds more physically wounded. Most recognized that over 10,000 troops in the area had suffered severe emotional trauma and would never view life the same way again. All will return home with a little less body or spirit. Their blood and sweat has been absorbed into the chaotic desert.

Although sporadic fighting was still underway, I was asked to enter this hellhole of a city. Insurrectionists remained at large and hundreds, if not thousands, of dead bodies littered the streets. Part of me wanted to refuse to go into the city, but I knew better. I would not be intimidated by the enemy. I would be well protected by Patrick and many Marines. However, I was deeply troubled for the young men who had just witnessed and survived the horrors of combat. The brutality of the fighting was the most severe American soldiers had experienced since the Vietnam War which occurred before many of them were even born.

Before leaving that Sunday morning, I celebrated Mass at 8:30 a.m. and led a quick class for sponsor training. Twenty-four candidates were preparing for the Sacraments of Initiation (Baptism, Confirmation and/or First Eucharist) into the Catholic Church. Each candidate had a sponsor, and classes were held every Tuesday. The process was a tremendous amount of work, but I managed thanks to RP1 Patrick Bowen. Although I was an officer and Patrick was enlisted, we bonded and offered excellent ministry together. Many people from my parish regularly prayed for Patrick by name. Even though Patrick was Methodist, he set up Catholic Masses in the camp and field correctly, with great care, respect and pride. Patrick also worked with my computer to provide music in the field. He even washed the altar linens, which was absolutely essential considering the number of Masses we provided. Being the chaplain and religious program specialist petty officer were lonely positions, and we often found great comfort in listening and sharing with each other.

When in camp, we always possessed a certain sense of security, even though a number of rockets and mortars had been launched there during the past eight months. Three men had been killed from such incidents which were mostly random shots. Whenever a mortar was launched from outside our camp, American forces immediately responded with fierce and devastating precision. At 10:00 a.m., we left the relative safety of our camp and departed for Fallujah City. Eighty percent of the structures in the city had been damaged from our bombings. These statistics did little to prepare me for what I encountered. The city remained incredibly dangerous, and the enemy had begun perfecting their IED's. I did not share with my family or friends back home that I would be going into the city, never mind on a regular basis. They were already petrified I was assigned within the Base Camp of Fallujah. I was supposed to remain in the camp at all times. My loved ones took great comfort in that fact, especially after hearing all of the terrifying news reports.

My armor-protected Humvee had four seats plus a spot for the gunner, which was the most dangerous of all jobs. The gunner stood between the two back seats which provided him with 360-degree access to a machine gun. So many gunners had been diced up and shredded upon their arrival at Bravo Surgical. When a gunner is hit, the two men in the back seats receive his blood. They must then take whatever action is needed to get to safety. This was quite intimidating. I prayed many rosaries in my seat. I often touched the Eucharist in my left-shoulder cargo pocket. Whether traveling to outlying posts or to the city of Fallujah, I always kept the Eucharist in this pocket. Since growing in my mother's womb, I have been in Church for the Sunday Mass. I missed only while on a ship at sea. The Mass could be in Swahili, Italian or Korean; I had always found a way to go. For me, when I am at Mass, I am home. Nothing means more to me.

Despite my trepidation, I was headed into the field to celebrate five Masses with the troops. On this particular morning, our group included Sergeant Skinner, Lance Corporal Nicholas Wood, First

Class Petty Officer Patrick Bowen, Chaplain Steve Pike (Regimental Chaplain, Episcopal), and myself. Approximately four vehicles were traveling in our convoy.

Chaplain Pike and I rode in the same vehicle because he sensed my great uneasiness with the whole event. However, I understood the importance of going into the city because as many as forty percent of the Marines were Catholic. They needed a Catholic priest. Steve hoped to secure my help for the upcoming weeks and months. I knew God wanted me there. Under no circumstances had I volunteered for this. Initially, I had emphatically refused to go into the city. But in the end, I believed in the mission and put my faith in God.

During the Vietnam War, a priest named Father Cappodano, the Grunt Padre, risked his life on the front lines. Some thought he was saintly, while others thought he was foolish. I continued to be the reluctant and complaining priest, although I was being healed quickly. My bishop, Victor Galeone, had sent me the story of a priest in the Korean War. This extremely heroic priest was a POW who had been tortured, yet he had eventually died. I realized this outcome was also a possibility for me, but I doubted I could ever be that brave and strong.

I would preside at five Masses in five different locations, with the last to occur at sunset. I wondered if the risk would be worth it with the battle still raging? The answer to my question trickled forth during the next few months and continues to come now, even as I write this story months later. This day absolutely ensured a connection of the roving priest for the Regiment, including Battalions 3-1, 3-5 and the Command Center under Colonel Michael Shupp.

In a military setting, I was an officer with all the respect due to the position. However, when the troops and I were engrossed in the Mass or the lightning-fast Communion service, I was their "Padre." The whole story of Exodus centers on the Ark of the Covenant, in which the Hebrew people believed God had pitched His tent among them. Marines view the padre as the presence of God among them. This is often true with chaplains of other denominations as well.

To achieve credibility, chaplains must be present and beside their men and women spiritually and physically during times of absolute terror, boredom and trials. The troops must sense we also experience the same smells of death, the sweat, the color of blood, loneliness, exhaustion, and hunger for peace. In the fields of training and battle are where Marines and soldiers most sense the presence of God and their need for Him. I disagree with the statement, "There are no atheists in foxholes." However, even the agnostic and atheists often sense something positive and hopefully profound in a chaplain among them. I felt very effective as the chaplain at Bravo Surgical Hospital.

When wounded Marines, sailors or soldiers arrived, I tried to discern their religious preference and talk to them on their level. I reminded them to breathe while the docs, nurses and corpsmen worked their magic. As I talked with them, I tried to offer comfort and assurance. I was always honest, within reason, if the injured asked about the status of one of their buddies. Sometimes, I simply said it was not in their best interest to discuss it at this time. I then shared the information when the injured could physically and mentally handle it. Basically, I acted as their family. I was their father and, in some sense, their mother, too.

Sometimes, other chaplains came into Bravo Surgical and were very unsure of themselves in the hospital and surgery setting. I tried to help them connect with the person in their spiritual charge. Doing this enabled me to move to other casualties. Sometimes, it was difficult for the chaplain to come in from the battlefield. He or she might be stationed at another camp where transportation was impossible. In those cases, I allowed the wounded person to invite me into the spiritual encounter. For Catholics, I was their Spiritual Father. We shared a very special connection of great love, although I never met any serviceman I didn't love. Many of their habits were annoying but completely bearable because I loved them all so much. Our experiences were phenomenal and joyful.

On the battlefield, I relied on the chaplain of each particular battalion to assist me in reaching Catholic men who needed my spiritual services. On this particular Sunday, I encountered an alarming fact in Fallujah. Many of the troops were numb and discombobulated. They had killed people and had witnessed their own friends' deaths. They had aged significantly. They were different. Their eyes communicated a level of intensity and dullness that was distressing.

First Mass

The first Mass was held in a house with a company from 3-5 Battalion. The location was just a few houses down from the scene of an infamous atrocity, the bridge from which burned U.S. contractors had been hung. In fact, our convoy parked right beside the bridge. I saw several dead cats, and the accompanying smell was horrendous. This battalion had arrived a week after me, and I hadn't been able to get to the men much before this time. I knew the other battalion quite well; however, I hadn't been able to 'pitch my tent' with this group yet, and I was initially greeted with indifference. Sadly, Chaplain Horn and I could not have prevented this. My time was stretched so thin, and I had not possessed enough strength to nurture the relationship.

The headquarters for this company was a typical Iraqi living room. Despite the initial apathy, three men were eager for Mass: Ed, Conrado and Anthony. As the service began, I removed my small green journal from my right-arm cargo pocket. I placed it on the makeshift altar so we could remember those who had died thus far. Our tiny congregation gathered. After Patrick set up the Mass with holy cards, medals, rosaries and candy, he left the room to ensure the surrounding area would remain fairly quiet. He also assured any latecomers it was okay to enter.

This first Mass in the city was the strangest. We heard bombing and shooting. The Company Commander could differentiate between friendly sounds and enemy ones. At any moment, another of his men could be wounded or killed. This was really tough. I prayed hard and furiously. Then a phantom bombshell hit me. When I solicited prayer petitions after the readings and mini homily, Conrado begged me to lift up his best friend, Victor Lu.

I was shaken, flushed and greatly disturbed.

Lance Corporal Victor Ronald Lu had come into Mortuary Affairs on November 13. I had already received six angels (KIA) that day. The Marines from Mortuary Affairs asked for me. I slowly walked into a tent attached to the refer (refrigerated morgue) for U.S. military service members. Before me, two gurneys rested upon four sawhorses. The Marines searched Victor's pockets for personal effects. As I waited, a terrible smell caused me to gag. Had I expected this, I would have put cologne below my nose, a technique I had learned while attending to the elimination needs of bedridden patients. I rarely prayed directly to Mary, the Mother of Jesus, but found myself begging her to help me survive this experience without getting sick. Victor had a tremendous wound to his head. I was already discouraged and somewhat depressed because of the great number of casualties and angels. This was just awful. I felt an overwhelming sadness as I sensed the enormity of Victor's sacrifice and the loss of his family. A Marine handed me a medal from Victor's pocket. It was the Miraculous Medal of Mary, the Mother of Jesus, wrapped carefully in cellophane. There was a tiny hole in the cellophane the size of a ballpoint pen's tip. As I looked closer, I realized the hole was actually located at the head of the medal, and Victor's blood was there.

As my head began to spin, I could have sworn I heard flying angels. The Marines bowed their heads while I prayed aloud. I sang the Ave Maria, which is the Hail Mary in Latin. During the song, the awful smell amazingly dissipated and became almost sweet and pleasant. I then recited the story of Jesus' arrival at the tomb of Lazarus. Jesus demanded the stone be rolled away. Martha, the dead man's sister, came to the Lord and said, "Master, surely there will be a stench; he has been dead for four days!" Jesus looked at Martha and said, "Martha, did I not tell you that if you believed, you would see the glory of God?" Then, Martha had them roll away the stone, and Lazarus came forward wrapped in burial bands with a cloth across his face. The people were stunned so Jesus had to say, "Untie him and let him go." Victor, too, had a cloth around his face.

As Catholics and Christians, it is our sure and certain hope that God offers us eternal life through Jesus. We always remember the dead at our Masses and pray that God will be merciful to them.

And so, I offered that Mass for Victor Ronald Lu in the city close to where he died. The Sacrifice of the Mass was so intense and comforting. Conrado's eyes flooded with tears. The tears kept coming. We were all totally present. I would not have chosen to be anywhere else in the entire universe. Although the moment was terrifying and heartbreaking, it was simultaneously glorious, joyful and heavenly. I thought of the dangers of the Breaking of Bread in Christian homes during horrendous times of persecutions. These feelings quickly evaporated, however, as we left that house for the next Mass.

21 November 2004: During the first Mass, our Humvee was parked beside the infamous bridge.

Victor Ronald Lu

The Second Mass

At the next location, I saw the Battalion Commander, Lieutenant Colonel Patrick Malay. I had encountered Pat at Bravo Surgical and at Masses on numerous occasions. Patrick is a very devout Catholic. He calls me simply 'Ron.' We developed a very close relationship forged during a terrifying war. Pat was like a father to his men and so was I to his Catholic men. I encouraged Pat to stay for Mass in this house, but he wasn't sure he had time. I said I could perform Mass in seven to ten minutes, and Patrick seemed to desperately need it. Gratefully, he agreed.

This was probably the quickest Mass of my life. Eleven other Marines crammed into that room around an altar made from cardboard boxes. I gave general absolution to all present considering the circumstances. Good thing I knew the Gospel by heart! The Mass was definitely valid. As I looked into each man's eyes, I was blown away by the most intense communication shared with just a glance. The men seemed to look deep into my being. I hope they saw Jesus inside me. Physically, I was standing, but spiritually, I was on my knees. I would have washed their feet with my tears. Maybe I did. We were even able to take Communion under both species (Body and Blood). Something beyond me happened. That Mass opened the door for a truly inspirational and healthy ministry to Battalion 3-5. Chaplain Dwight Horn and I soon provided a profound ministry to his battalion centered on sincere friendship. I later discovered Chaplain Horn had laid one of his hands on George Payton (the amputee with the tear) as George was evacuated from the battlefield and flown to Bravo Surgical just before his death. Ministry was always a team effort coupled with great compassion. It was as if Jesus was there with them, and he was.

The Third Mass

En route to the Combat Control Center, we threw candy to children standing on the side of the road. There were only a few of them, but in this place of gunfire and bombs, there were way too many. These were poor ones who hadn't the means to evacuate when warned. Many people had sent me care packages with candy, so I had plenty to share. However, the children stepped too close to the convoys, and I was so afraid they would be hurt.

At the Command Center in the middle of the city, we trekked through a yard that looked as if it had once been a playground. Colonel Shupp was leaving by convoy to visit the various companies throughout the city. The war had obviously taken a toll on this courageous man who had lost a number of his men in the regiment. He didn't have time for Mass because of his incredible concern for his men. As I stood in the doorway and began to remove my helmet, I turned and left the others, including my bodyguard. I called to Colonel Shupp.

"Colonel!"

"Yes, Father?"

"Michael, would you like to receive Communion?"

The intensity shone in the eyes of this truly great man. I could only begin to imagine what he had experienced both physically and morally. His anguish and pain were apparent. I said I could forgive his sins. It is rare to see that kind of hunger for the Eucharist. The Colonel possessed true remorse. "Forgiven!"

"The Body of Christ, Michael."

"Amen!"

Then the Sergeant Major nearby asked for the same two Sacraments. Humbling.

We entered the five-story building that we would visit frequently during the next three months. Patrick and I set up for Sunday Mass. These guys were definitely roughing it. Most of the men had various assignments during the day, so only three men showed up for Mass. One of them was the driver of my Humvee. This was not good because it meant I would soon be asked to venture into Fallujah at night. This would really stretch my 'fear factor.'

John, Nick, James and I celebrated Mass on the second floor. In the weeks to come, the average amount of men in attendance would be fifteen to twenty. I used my computer for two songs. The music added a little flair to such dull surroundings. During this small service, all four of us experienced a kind of charismatic state. We weren't waving our hands or shouting or anything like that. The experience took place within our spirits. Personally, I felt suspended and overwhelmingly happy and content. The others shared similar feelings.

The Fourth Mass

We set off in our convoy for 3-1 Battalion companies. I had become great friends with Chaplain Ron Kennedy over the past months. His battalion had a company at Abu Ghraib prison. His company commander was also Catholic. Ron had given me valuable insight regarding the city of Fallujah. His Battalion had been there for about seven months. When Ron and his RP shared pictures of venturing into the city, I was shocked and impressed. I would have been too terrified. And here I was today…still pretty scared! I had been regularly lifting up prayers for my beloved chaplain friend, Ron, for the past two weeks. I was afraid something had happened to him. Many of his men had already come through Bravo Surgical (some in body bags), and I had only been able to get "sketchy" information about Ron's well-being from the wounded and those who brought them in.

Upon seeing Ron at the command post in a flour factory, I was overwhelmingly relieved. Spontaneously, I embraced him. He was really glad to see me. He had prepared the Catholic men well for my arrival. I was overjoyed that forty men attended the Mass with yet another altar made from boxes. Ron held a Protestant service at the same time. The Mass had great reverence, intensity and tears. These men had lived through hell and had suffered a forty percent loss of their men to death and injuries. They were genuinely happy to see me and, most importantly, thanked God for keeping them safe.

Although these men have had a deep spiritual experience, it might be years before they fully return to the Church and the Sacraments. Many never really had strong faith formation. A large number expressed a desire to turn their lives around, but the call of this world is often too much to overcome. Many are like St. Augustine who said, "Convert me, Lord, but not yet!" Possessions, pleasures (especially those of a sexual nature) and peer pressure are too much for 18 to 24 year olds who were taught neither morality nor ethics. And yet, after one young man received a religious medal, he meditated briefly and exclaimed, "Father, I will never take it off!" Another man had been struggling with his emotions after witnessing many deaths and horrendous wounds among his fellow Marines. After our Mass, he said, "Jesus is having his way with me..."

The Fifth and Final Mass of the Day

As darkness approached, our final stop was the train station. I was truly exhausted from carrying so much weight, both physical and spiritual. The sun was setting, and Chaplain Ron Kennedy stayed with us at the station. All of the men I had seen on this day hadn't been able to shower in about two weeks. Each man probably slept with one eye open. So when Mass began in a little tent, just one man attended. His name was Nathan Schmidt. Nathan was one of the nicest guys around. His spirit was incredibly gentle, kind and strong at the same time. Nathan didn't strike me as a typical Marine, yet he also seemed to be an absolutely wonderful

Marine officer. He was wrestling with the decision of whether to get married or to become a priest. Either way, his life will be wonderful. I met Nathan the first week after my arrival in Fallujah. He knew Major Kevin Shea quite well and was present at Kevin's last Mass. Kevin even taught Nathan at the Naval Academy.

I invited Chaplain Ron Kennedy to attend Mass. Although Ron couldn't receive the Eucharist, it was truly a profound moment. I long for all Christian faiths to come together and worship Jesus as one people.

Then we returned to the MEK (Main Fallujah Camp). I wrote the following in my small green journal:

Long Day, Long Love, Long Suffering! Good Night!

Chaplains Ron Kennedy, Steve Pike, and me just before the fifth Mass

22 November 2004 Saint Cecelia

My parents were married on this date. Their union in the Sacrament with God's blessing bore me as fruit. They didn't know the path their lives would take. Very few, if any of us, can fathom the depths and heights and despair and joy of a relationship, a journey taken by two. My mom and dad were married for 48 years in this world before my mother's death. Their courtship was a brief two years as they became acquainted and fell in love. My father adored my mother. She was a real lady. When Mom died, their marriage died. Often I speak of missing my mom, but rarely do I grieve the death of their love. Their loving partnership lasted nearly fifty years... a long time for today's world. But it was too short for those who knew them, especially their nine children and more than twenty grandchildren.

My father has since remarried and is quite happy. I am quite happy as well. Nancy is a remarkable woman, nurse and beloved lady. She is a mother for me in my mother's absence. And yet I receive her for all eternity as an important part of my life. I know my mom rejoices with me. Nancy always writes to me and shares our love for the Lord, Our God. She reads the Bible daily.

I feel my mother's true presence with me in Iraq. In a way, she called me out of my comfort zone to tend "her boys" in my journey through the war-torn streets of Fallujah. When Mom was ill and undergoing outpatient surgery for her cancer, she unselfishly sent me to visit other patients in the recovery room with various physical and spiritual problems.

I pause amidst the intensity of this war zone to be grateful for my parents coming together in love to bear me, support me, and love me, united by God in love. My parents were my first and most important teachers of faith. Without their love for God, I wouldn't be here in this time and place. Life is full of so many surprises, twists, and turns. The pulse of life is strong, and Jesus heals deeply, eternally, and profoundly.
O to be alive in Love!!

\+ **Michael Ryan Cohen** – Jewish (angel prayer card)

25 November 2004 Thanksgiving

The wounded have been arriving on a daily basis. I speak with practically everyone who comes through Bravo Surgical. If they are Catholic, I offer the Sacraments of Anointing and Communion and Reconciliation. Other Christians share their faith with me and ask for help as they try to understand their confusion. I continue to record names in my green notebook. On Thanksgiving, all the chaplains participated in a morning celebration together. We recently welcomed a female Lutheran chaplain who brings another beautiful dimension to the overall ministry in Iraq.

In the evening, we ate a delicious dinner at the chow-hall. We even got to drink two real beers rather than the non-alcoholic stuff!

Although alcohol was not allowed in Iraq, many of the troops were creative and had friends and family send it in packages. I wondered how some of these guys and gals deprived themselves of alcohol for over six months. I did not observe many abuses or problems, though.

As I ate my last few bites, I was alerted that several men were coming into Bravo Surgical. I stood and quickly ran there. Six men arrived. One of them was a Catholic who told me his mother was an Atheist. This story was truly sad and heart-wrenching. Another of the injured was Gunny Javier Obleas. I anointed him and talked with him as the doctors prepared him to be evacuated. He spoke of his wife, Kim, and daughter, Lena. He was Catholic and very receptive to the Sacraments. *I learned he died a week later in Germany on December 1. This war stinks.

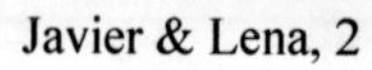

Javier & Lena, 2 Kim & Lena Lena, 5

May 16, 2008

Hello Father Ron,

I just wanted to let you know that I received your email. I ordered your book as soon as I read your message.

Lena and I are doing very well. Lena will be turning 5 on May 20th. She has grown so fast and looks just like her daddy, Javier Obleas. We are still living in Texas.

I am now on the Board of Directors for Schertz Humane Society. I love to rescue animals… take care of them, foster them and find them forever homes. After Javier passed away I threw myself into the humane society here in Schertz. I enjoy what I do and Lena loves the puppies. Javier always loved animals and I always wanted to be a Veterinarian… so this is my way of doing what I enjoy but still being a stay at home MOM... :0)

I have met a wonderful man named Raul. He is wonderful and a great father figure to Lena. His faith in the LORD is like no other I have seen. His brother, Michael Hernandez has been in a coma for 13 yrs... He was hit by a drunk driver. Raul's mother and father take care of Michael 24/7 and Raul is his physical therapist. As a family they decided that they would take care of him instead of putting him in a rehab clinic. They are a strong family but I pray for their strength. Please pray for them Father Ron. Raul's Father is a Marine Corp Veteran.

Thank you for all that you do!

Kim Obleas

Please keep in contact and keep me posted on how you are doing.

God Bless you!

Here is a picture of Javier… this is right before he left for Fallujah... 2004 (Picture on previous page)

26 November 2004 **Friday**

+ **David Houk** - *"Piercer" was listed as his religion*

+ **Bradley Faircloth** *(his religion was listed as no religious preference) He had a St. Christopher Medal that was gold like Senator Kerry wore in Vietnam.*

He went on mission trips with his mother to Jamaica and Africa.

The Potato Factory

The Potato Factory was originally just that - a potato factory. But now, while one refrigerator still contained potatoes, the next one housed dead bodies. Most of the bodies were already decomposing. Marines from Mortuary Affairs had pleaded with me to come celebrate Mass at this location where they were assigned. It was one of the most gruesome sights I had ever encountered. Over four-hundred bodies were unclaimed. It was like a mass grave before the burial. I couldn't imagine trying to claim a body. I doubt I could have handled the stench to search for my own loved one. People's entire lives were just tossed into one big room. Most of the dead were probably poor Iraqi people unable to escape their unfortunate circumstances. Many were likely murdered by insurrectionists. I gagged and fought an uncontrollable urge to throw up. Approximately twenty Marines and one chaplain lived within this structure. As I quickly observed my grotesque surroundings, I imagined hell could be like this.

Patrick and I had traveled by convoy to visit the potato factory late in the afternoon on the day after Thanksgiving. As of 11:00 p.m., we were still there before finally securing return transportation. We rode on the back of an unprotected open-air truck on a cold night. Our unappealing alternative would have been to stay at the potato factory overnight. Unfortunately, our driver (a confident Marine officer) got lost on the way back to Camp Fallujah. We drove completely around the outside wall. After awhile, we were no longer even on a road. Patrick looked nervous as he scoped everything in sight on the moonlit night. My heart pumped rapidly. I thought of all the wounded who had been bludgeoned by IED's and imagined what it would be like for those in Bravo Surgical to discover their own chaplain on a trauma bed or in Mortuary Affairs. The possibility of an IED or friendly fire was dangerously real.

The miserable journey was nearly unbearable. Patrick and I only wanted to do our jobs, but we were stuck driving in circles in some sand-blasted version of the Twilight Zone. As the truck bounced all over the place, I lay back and longingly gazed at the clear and cold sky. Suddenly, I felt overwhelmingly safe and loved by God. The situation was beyond my control, and God gave me comfort. I was more fortunate than the hundreds of people in those horrid, barely refrigerated rooms at the potato factory. I was luckier than the poor Marines and sailors living in that hellhole. I could not complain. We had survived thus far. God wasn't done with us yet.

Our earlier celebration of the Eucharist now made sense. I was not alone. During that Mass, the awful smell of our surroundings seemed crushed by the fragrance of God. The fifteen young men were so appreciative I was there. They had been unable to attend Mass for weeks and did not expect me. At the end of Mass, one of the Marines beamed with a smile from ear to ear as he tearfully embraced me. He and another Marine had sought me out during the Thanksgiving dinner and begged me to come out. In fact, Patrick and I had previously tried to travel to the potato factory, but our attempts to secure transportation had always failed. On Thanksgiving, I had promised the men if God opened the door, Patrick and I would be there on Friday. We had successfully made it! The men loved all of the religious articles and gifts. Mostly, however, they just appreciated my visit, even if I couldn't pitch my tent. I was humbled again.

As we continued to travel in the back of our hopelessly lost and unprotected truck, I slowly relaxed and savored the taste of the Body and Blood of Jesus. I thought, if God is for us, who can be against us? We eventually returned to Camp Fallujah, albeit very late. However, I was becoming emotionally worn-out and physically drained. The weekend was just beginning, and I was scheduled for seven more Masses. I would also be available for the hospital. God give me strength!

27 November 2004 **Saturday**

The Marines and sailors were so weary of this battle. Late at night, I often wandered into the wards and made myself present and available to them. A Marine, sailor or soldier was always in need of a father's love. Even non-Catholics wanted to talk to me. The men and women in the wards either waited for a helicopter to transport them out of the area or they returned to the battlefield. An outstanding priest had been attached to the Division, but he had returned home after only a month when his mother died.

Thankfully, the stream of casualties slowed during the next two months. I drastically increased my number of Masses and often traveled to the troops. I took great pride in the ongoing process of preparing twenty-four servicemen for the sacraments. Patrick and I were constantly in motion. We provided over nine Masses per weekend and a ministry of presence that stretched us to our limits. The wounds to the psyches and souls of our men and women were mounting.

+ **Joshua Lucero** *(Christian, Cross in my pocket, oldest of seven, prayed with his friends Paul and James)*

+ **Kirk Bussleman** *(Christian, 72nd Angel for me, prayer)*

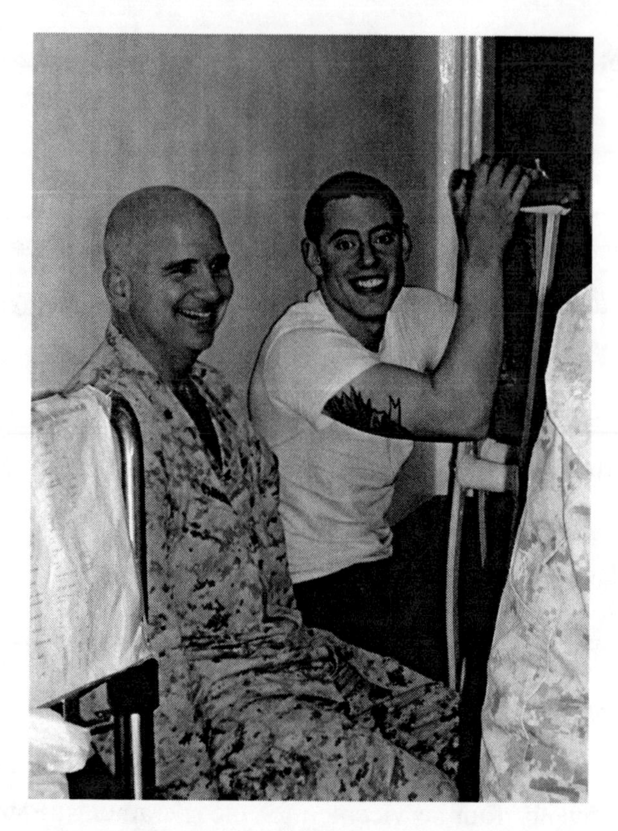

Steve Kephart and me in the hallway of Bravo Surgical during a calm moment

28 November 2004 First Sunday of Advent

I celebrated Mass at the base theater at 8:30 a.m. While Patrick and I waited for our convoy, two Catholics arrived at Bravo Surgical with serious injuries. One man eventually died. I anointed both of them.

I stepped outside behind Bravo Surgical to drink a cup of coffee. A young Marine, Edward Flak, sat waiting to be picked up by his unit. Edward said, "Aren't you Father Ron?" After catching me off guard, he smiled and said I had been an associate priest at Sacred Heart Church in Jacksonville when he was in the sixth grade. I had even taught his class a number of times! The kid cracked me up and made me smile. I disliked the thought of him returning to battle…this young boy who had been my student. Edward even worried about *me* as I prepared to go into the city in a few minutes.

November was such a painfully intense month. Our service members will be unpacking the baggage of their wounded souls for many years. It could possibly take a lifetime for some to come to grips with their traumatic experiences. There would be no more deaths in November, thank God!

Army Chaplain Sorenson and "the Padre" just after Mass. The Army had no Catholic priest for the Battle of Fallujah. 10,000 troops and one padre; God will provide…Lord, have mercy!

Chapter VIII
DECEMBER in FALLUJAH

(Advent of Peace)

On the last day of November, Patrick and I took a helicopter to Al Taqaadam Camp (TQ) to celebrate the Chaplain Corps anniversary for a couple of days. Nearly three months earlier, we had survived the convoy going to Fallujah; this departing flight would have to be somewhat safer. Once airborne, however, I reconsidered the wisdom of this trip. The helicopter was extremely loud. The night was eerily dark. Fortunately, we arrived at TQ safely, though. The break from regular duties was so refreshing.

On the return flight to Fallujah, Patrick and I sat in the back of the helicopter alone. The night air was freezing. Unfortunately, our helicopter was surveying the city of Fallujah on this night. I was nervous and cold, and I really needed to urinate. I hadn't expected the flight to take an entire hour, and my bladder felt as if it was going to burst. During the staff meeting the next day, I told everyone I was glad to be 'home.'

The Liturgical Season of Advent was upon us. We even planned a Penance service, and three priests flew in for it. My brother priests had doubted the additional need until our service on December 21, a Tuesday evening. Over fifty troops availed themselves of the Sacrament of Reconciliation. Reconciliation was so important, especially for the twenty-four candidates who were preparing for full initiation into the Church.

I didn't journal much during this time. The month of November and the Battle for Fallujah had completely wiped me out. There was little time to breathe. I was exhausted. I was losing about two pounds each week and celebrating an increased number of Masses. The psychological and spiritual fallout from the war was overwhelming, as was the steady flow of patients. The most tragic days were December 12, 23, and 28. Although Christmas Day was rainy, cold and depressing, it truly ended up being "the best Christmas ever."

Prayer comes natural to me. In Iraq, prayer was more important to me than food. For the first time in my life, I fasted for twenty-four hours two days a week. Often, I wasn't even hungry at the completion of this discipline. I wasn't fanatical or anything like that. Fasting just seemed like the right thing to do at the time. It was like being in a purification mode. Since my return from Iraq, I still fast and eat no solid food for twenty-four hours almost every week. I do not lose weight. In fact, I may have gained! To me, fasting is a gift I can give to my Beloved God. It becomes amazingly habit-forming in a relatively short time. Fasting helps me appreciate not only food but also all of the wonderful simple pleasures of living on Earth.

At 5:00 a.m., Mortuary Affairs awoke me. A member of the 9th Communication Unit had been killed in a vehicle accident. The unit couldn't locate its chaplain. Until now, this company hadn't lost a Marine to death the entire deployment. The situation was very sad. Lance Corporal In Chul Kim had been in a seven-ton truck as the gunner. These trucks were used to transport many troops and heavy equipment. A young Marine driver had inadvertently taken a turn too fast. The truck had flipped, killing Kim instantly. I prayed over Kim's body. The leadership of the Marine's unit then begged me to talk to those struggling with the reality of his death.

As I walked to their unit on a very cold morning, I quickly tried to shake the grogginess of sleep out of my eyes. I scoured my mind for what I knew about the situation. I was so grateful for the hundred yards to be alone. The unit had requested me because I had previously helped them with two Red Cross messages. (Red Cross messages are notification to a service member of a death or emergency crisis at home.) They liked my style. By this time, most of the camp personnel knew me as the only 'Padre' on the base.

Upon my arrival at the unit, I was escorted to a tent. I expected a few Marines. However, I encountered approximately fifty men and women in a truly depressed and angry mood. I was absolutely at a loss of what I should say or do. The deceased Marine had not been particularly religious, and while I remembered him, I hadn't known him well at all. However, after being a chaplain for over fifteen years, I had been called to pray 'generic' many times. So, I started with Taps.

I was frank with the group and asked each of them to share one word to describe Kim. Somehow, their intense grief, anger, depression, and confusion seemed to lessen. Their emotions had been lanced, and their tears were allowed to drain. Some of the guys had not cried since leaving their loved ones at home. They were still true Marines and kept their composure. I was so groggy and tired that God was better able to use me as a conduit of His love. I certainly didn't give them candy-coated theological pie-in-the-sky hope. I managed as well as I could, and I sensed that was all they needed or wanted. In my own vulnerability, I was raw and weepy. I grieved for Lance Corporal In C. Kim, and I grieved for the lost innocence of the entire unit as they faced their first death. All present died a little that morning. I died a little more. I felt really old. Most of the Marines could be my own sons or daughters. I remained strong but felt myself inching closer to the breaking point.

I walked back to Bravo Surgical Hospital. The sun would rise in less than an hour, but I couldn't sense that. I was crushed with the darkness enveloping my soul. I left a message for the chaplain of Kim's unit explaining what had happened. I also left a message for my supervisory chaplain that he would have to cover Bravo Surgical for the day. I climbed into my cot and didn't wake until the afternoon. The whole damn war would have to go on without me. My pain was almost unbearable. I am not sure a bomb could have roused me.

I hadn't written anything in my journal since November 22. I was visiting patients in the wards, going out to do Masses and checking on injured men and women in the trauma units. Sadly, I had even stopped writing names in my green journal. I must have been numb. I was teaching classes on Tuesday evenings, counseling, preparing for and celebrating Masses, attending staff meetings two or three times a week, and looking ahead to Christmas in Fallujah. I called home every couple of days or at least once a week. I prayed every day for an hour or two. My responsibilities seem overwhelming when I recall that time. RP1 Patrick Bowen was exhausted, too.

Navigating the Ship of the Soul
Every holy day is a possibility of a holy war.

One moment yet, a little while,
and I will shake the heavens and the earth,
the sea and the dry land.
Greater will be the future glory of this house
than the former;
And in this house I will give peace,
says the Lord of hosts!
The Prophet Haggai 2:6, 9

This quote from the prophet Haggai seemed relevant because I thought God had been a little slow with his promise. Maybe I just thought the "moments" were excruciatingly long.

9 December 2004 **CHRISTOPHER**

Christopher Adelsperger arrived dead from wounds he received in an ambush. Haven't had many angels these past days. And then I am pulled back into this craziness. He was only nineteen.

+ Adelsperger, Christopher: "Christian"

He was pronounced dead after arrival. 3-5 Marines

(Prayer and Anointing)

10 December 2004 **Friday**

I celebrated Mass with the Army.

It all came too fast for me to record.

11 December 2004

+ Greg Rund, LCPL, 3-5 Marines: *(shot in the head)*

+ Christopher Adelsperger

+ Greg Rund

Third Sunday of Advent

– Death is all around me!

Our Lady of Guadalupe

I am quickly fading as I try to pen a thought or two before I die to this day. It is about seven minutes prior to midnight. Twenty wounded and six angels came into Bravo Surgical. I received four angels (KIA) and prayed for one at Mass. In the midst of all this deadly horror, we celebrated the sacrificial Lamb of God. Nothing is more important than the God of all creation, the One and Only God who lives among us.

So today, I prayed. We prayed. We celebrated one Mass in the morning and another two Masses outside the base and in the City of Fallujah. I also brought Communion to the men on watch at various outposts. When I returned to Bravo Surgical, the wounded were coming. The dead were coming. Joy to sorrow and back to joy and then sorrow is the usual routine around here. I wish I could wrap Jesus as a gift and give him to others. There are so many who are unaware of Jesus, the all-forgiving and loving God with us. So many have not experienced the Holy Spirit.

The evil one roams. Jesus said once the devil leaves a person, he wanders the world and finds no one and nowhere to go, so he returns to that person and tries to get back in him or her. If the devil can't gain entry, he retrieves seven other devils and returns to infect the person worse than before.

This is getting ugly.

+ **Jeffery Kirk:** *3-5 Marines*

+ **Ian Stewart:** *Christian, 3-5 Marines*

+ **Melvin Blazer:** *Staff Sgt, Baptist, 3-5 Marines*

+ **Hilario Lopez:** *Catholic, special prayer, 3-5 Marines*

+ **Jason Clariday:** *3-5 Marines*

+ **Joshua Dickenson:** *3-1 Marines, Jesus Prayer*

It was a late night of horror as the Lieutenant Colonel and his Sergeant Major watched helplessly as one after another of their men arrived either injured or dead. My anger almost overflowed. The injured included Matthew, Chris, Adam, Jason, John, Wilson, David, Brandon, Daniel, Kyle, Noah, Charlie, Joshua, and Christopher. Most were Christian and desired prayer. Some were downright numb.

Lieutenant Colonel Patrick Malay was becoming a friend forged on the Eucharist in the battlefield. Amazingly, Jesus made his presence known at this ugly time. I doubt I will ever understand the significance of that night. I didn't know how much more I could take, but I didn't let anyone know this. Thank God it was nearly the last gruesome day.

SPEECHLESS

One evening, there was a horrific blast. One of the Marines was not physically injured but was unable to speak. The nurses thought his injury might be spiritual, so I was notified. After attending to all of the other casualties, including a number of deaths, I took some time with the young man. He had suffered a concussion. He was unresponsive except for his eyes, so I communicated with him by writing on a prescription note pad. (See page 268) I still have the three pieces of paper in which I recorded our dialogue.

Me: What is your name?

Chris: Lcpl Christopher __________.

Me: I am Father Ron. Were you near the blast?

Chris: Yes. Behind the 7-ton in the Humvee.

Me: What is your faith? I am a Catholic Priest.

Chris: Christian.

Me: Would you like a St. Christopher Medal with the Marine emblem on the other side?

Chris: Yes

Me: I will get it. 5 min.

Me: Married?

Chris: No

Me: Children?

Chris: Yes, Makayla going to be 2.

She is not really mine, but I raised her.

Me: Where were you born? How old?

Chris: Oddessa TX 20

Me: Did you help move the injured or dead?

Chris: Yes

Me: What else besides your hearing is hurting?

Chris: My head and my speech is not so good.

Me: Spirit & heart?

Chris: Yes

Me: Jesus always asked people, "What do you want me to do for you?"

Chris: help me

Me: Did you attend Church much?

Chris: Not since I joined the military.

Me: How long will you be in the Marine Corps?

Chris: almost 2 yrs

Me: What can I help you with?

Chris: You can pray with me

Me: <u>My honor.</u>

(We prayed together. He could hear me and responded to my voice.)

Me: Give me a few minutes to get the medal. I will be right back.

Chris: OK

I have no further evidence of our conversation. He started talking to both the doctor and me once I gave him the St. Christopher Medal.

Christopher was a very typical Marine confronted with war. As I grew up, I often wondered what a real war situation would be like. Once I got there, though, war was in color and not black and white. War was not only something a person could see, but also something to feel and experience intensely within the soul. After leaving the hospital, I wept.

16 December 2004 — Fasting in Fallujah

Yesterday, I fasted. God knows that I am weak when fasting. My longings and desires are sometimes more for food rather than for the Bread of Eternal Life. O yes, I love the Lord with all my heart, soul and being. My impulses and addictive personality just want to reach for something other than my Beloved Lord.

Yesterday, beginning at midnight, I halfheartedly attempted to fast; I thought and believed I was doing something for God.

However, it was God encouraging me all along, longing for me to step out in faith, but I did not know. God is Father and Mother to me and loves all of us into eternity. God holds out his hands while He holds us up. God pleads for us to walk across the room. He rejoices in our wobbly, weak, insecure and first steps.

For the Lord does not see as man sees;
for man looks at the outward appearance,
but the Lord looks at the heart. – 1 Samuel 16:7

With great love, God watched over me as I tried to go without food for 24 hours. I wanted to better understand God. We are just children, babes in arms. God desires our friendship. God is not out to get us. God is Jesus, who came down to play and dance and sing and cry and live with us TODAY! Toward evening, I felt I had adequately fasted, and food was plenty. I wrestled with thoughts. I observed others eating and living, and I felt like an outsider. Actually, I was within the Sacred Heart of Jesus, but I did not realize it. I succumbed to cups of tea, knowing that someday I will fast without water. Recently, I fasted without water during Rosh Hashanah at the encouragement of the visiting rabbi.

I awoke in the morning and was hungry, yet I wasn't. I wanted to do Morning Prayer immediately but then decided to first head to the chow hall for breakfast. I almost heard Jesus say, "Come, have breakfast!" So, I somewhat succeeded in a 24-hour fast. God cheered my baby step. O Jesus, teach us to walk. Teach us to run with you, to race with you. O Jesus, I want to dance forever in your love, your peace, and for all eternity.

17 December 2004

St. Michael protect us and bring us Home

I have to share this story with you. A kid named Matthew, a lance corporal, was at Bravo Surgical on Nov 11. I noticed his beautiful St. Michael Medal. I asked him if he was Catholic, and he was. The medal's chain was broken, so I told Matthew I would find something with which to connect it. Only then did he relinquish his prized possession to the priest. I felt honored. He was in bad shape in the trauma room; blood was everywhere. I anointed him with the oils of the sick and prayed as if Matthew was my own son. Then, I ran to the supply people and procured a cord. Upon my return to trauma, he was already in the operating room, and two angels suddenly arrived in the tanks. We had to somehow unload them. One of the angels was Catholic, and I administered last rites. I also tended to the poor guys who delivered the angels. They were dazed. I eventually gave communion to four of them and anointed them because of the horror they had just experienced. One of them was considering the priesthood and was overwhelmingly grateful for Communion. His last Mass had been three weeks earlier. I was on my knees because of their strong faith and how they ministered to each other.

Once those men (brave and courageous heroes) had emotionally stabilized, I heard the choppers whizzing and remembered the St. Michael medal in my cargo pocket. I ran into Bravo Surgical and saw the back door open, which meant the ambulance had brought Matthew to the landing pad for evacuation. It was a beautiful, sunny late afternoon. My inner being, however, was very dark. I silently promised this Marine I would find a way to return his precious medal. I ran down the street like the Merciful Father (Luke 15:11-32) greeting his son who was returning home...The landing pad was about 200 yards away. But I was too late. I knew his name, Matthew Brown, but that was about all I knew. For over a month, I carried his medal in my pocket every day. At night, I put it on my bedpost. There were four names inscribed on the back: Sarah, Rachel, Benjamin, and Matthew.

I urged Patrick to help me find Matthew Brown's address and telephone number. I had recently tried a number that was supposed to be Matthew's mother, but the number had been out of order. Then, the Commandant of the Marine Corps visited us about a week ago. He talked about visiting the wounded at Bethesda, as did the Secretary of the Navy a week before that. (Interestingly, I gave the Secretary of the Navy a St. Christopher Medal with the Navy emblem on the back after he gave me one of his coins.) I had wanted to ask the Commandant and the Secretary of the Navy if either of them could return the medal to Matthew, but I had resisted.

Yesterday, I finally reached Matthew Brown's mother in Carlisle, Pennsylvania. I didn't want my phone call to spook her in case Matthew had died. I asked if Matthew was there, and she said, "He is sleeping." I was so relieved Matthew was alive. He had been recovering at Bethesda Naval Hospital in rehab and was learning how to walk. I didn't ask if he had lost a leg. I told Matthew's mother about his medal and what had happened, and she gasped. When the Commandant of the Marine Corps presented him his Purple Heart he had said, "Sir, this is really nice, but what I really want is my St. Michael Medal back. Can you help me get it?"

Matthew's mother ran to get her son. It was very early in the morning in Carlisle. She said, "He wants desperately to talk with you, Father."

Matthew got on the phone, and we talked and shared. He was so respectful and pleasant. I could tell that recovery was sometimes slow and painful. I asked Matthew about the three other names on the back of the medal. His brother, Benjamin, and two close friends had been in a tragic car accident, and the medal was crafted in their honor. They were grateful for the protection of St. Michael. I teared up upon hearing this story. I then asked Matthew for his e-mail address for future correspondence, and it was 'saxman.' He plays the tenor sax which is what I play and own. O God, O God is so good!

Today, I packed the medal in a box and sent it home. This sounds weird, but I miss the medal a little bit. I also tucked in four holy cards of St. Michael from my friend, Father Jeff, along with a St. Christopher medal with the Navy's emblem on the back. I had these medals, thanks to Barbara Crawford and the Knights of Columbus from my hometown. Ah, the joy of life!

I shared the story with the staff and surgeons of Bravo Surgical this morning. They suggested I write to the Commandant and report that the request of a Marine has been accomplished. We shall see.

Chapter IX
Seven Christians

December 23, 2004

This is the story about seven Christians. Six belong to various flavors of Christianity; one is Catholic. I met all of the men around the same time on Camp Fallujah, Iraq, during the Battle of Fallujah.

Two Humvees slammed into the parking lot of Bravo Surgical Hospital. Philip was dropped at the front entrance as his shoulder bled profusely. After the quick stop, the vehicles then drove the short distance to Mortuary Affairs.

At the time, I did not notice Eddie, Quincy and Brandon, as I was focused on receiving the dead angels. These three men carefully unloaded their fallen shipmates and friends whose dog tags read: 'Baptist,' 'Christian,' and 'No Preference.' At this point, only last names were available, so I did an initial prayer for each man as the bodies lay on the plywood floor.

First, I received Raleigh whose dog tag read 'Christian.' He lay atop a black body bag on a stretcher raised off the floor by two sawhorse supports. The other two angels had been temporarily placed in the refer trailer at the end of the tent.

The Marines of Mortuary Affairs were incredibly sensitive and caring individuals. They always welcomed me for every 'angel,' recognizing the physical and spiritual dignity of each body before them. When I was ready to pray, they immediately paused and respectfully bowed their heads. They were like cherubs of heaven assisting me in every way and noticing the holy presence surrounding the dead. Although Raleigh was the 76th angel I had personally received, the experience still felt like my first time. He died in action, but life still remained in him. It's hard to explain. Life isn't done until God, his Father, says so. I am an ordained priest of God forever, according to the order of Melchizedek. I am Ron Moses. And so with God, my Father, your Father, and Our Father watching, I beheld God's son, Raleigh.

I don't remember exactly how or what I prayed, but my prayer was genuine, intense, and glorious. This was the only place on earth I could be and remain at peace. God placed me here at this time, and I was not going to fight Him. God called me out of my slumber of self-centeredness to offer this beloved child, this son, this man to Him. I stripped Raleigh of his sins and let them all fall to the dirt with the authority invested in me by Jesus. Mary, the Mother of God, and our Mother, felt the thorns of this tragic and violent death in her Sacred Heart. She wept. God wept. Jesus wept. I wept. The Marines wept.

The LORD is good to those who wait for Him,

to the soul who seeks Him.

Lamentations 3:25

When I left the tent and walked into the sunshine, I sensed I was within a cloud of intense grief. Eddie, Quincy and Brandon were gathered in horror, confusion, fear, and anxiety. They were gripped with grief and shock. In their own arms, they had carried their comrades, friends, and fellow Marines to this temporary morgue. Cigarettes wobbled in their shaking hands.

I felt a spiritual nudge from Mary, the Mother of Jesus, urging me to act: "Go on. Comfort my children." I quickly ascertained they were all Christians of various denominations. We invoked Jesus in breath and in word. We prayed, listened, and shed many tears for Raleigh, Eric and James. Our prayer was somewhat awkward on the outside but just perfect as an offering to God. We were brothers of Jesus, and God our Father accepted our prayer and love. "These are my beloved sons with whom I am well pleased."

Within minutes, the spiritual cloud and darkness cleared. The moment was very special. These young men gave me the courage and strength to now offer the other two to their God and Father.

I returned to Philip, the Catholic of the group, who had likely suffered a broken shoulder from a gunshot wound. Philip was feisty, to say the least, yet warm as they come. Raised in the Bronx, he was a diehard Yankees fan. Being from Boston, I thanked God the Red Sox had finally beaten the Yankees this year! They had miraculously progressed to the World Series and won it for the first time in 86 years. Diversions were necessary in Iraq in order to survive the intensity of war.

As Philip's tears ran down his face, I cleaned his dirt-caked teeth. The raw, exposed red flesh of Philip's arm made me a bit queasy, but I pushed the feelings aside. I gently wet Philip's mouth. When headed to surgery, the wounded were not allowed to drink any water beforehand. I anointed Philip and forgave his sins. There was absolutely no guile in Philip. Albeit gruff and rough, Philip could charm the devil or even a Red Sox fan. He was stocked with all the religious medals and paraphernalia for protection. His faith was elementary and probably stronger than most theologians. I imagined the wars he possibly experienced in his childhood family. In some ways, his present life was no different. Philip and I wept for his Marine brothers who had died. He was determined to return to his platoon. Philip is the kind of guy who could storm Heaven with his faith and cause healing. He would return to his platoon.

I walked back to the tent to receive two more angels. I passed Eddie, Quincy and Brandon. They respectfully stood nearby while I did whatever a "professional prayer" was supposed to do for their friends. I sensed they were praying for their friends and for me in this ugly and devastating dimension of war. I was truly grateful for their heroic lives full of prayer, love, and protection.

Near Raleigh, I encountered the body and aura of James, a lance corporal, whose dog tag simply read 'No Preference.' I knew in my heart he was Christian because of my conversation with the others and by his name, James. James' body seemed coated with his blood. One of the duties of the Mortuary Affairs' Marines was to search the body for all wounds and identifiable marks. The doctor or surgeon was usually present and prepared the report which had a front and back outline of a body. James had no personal effects to define his faith except an illegible card covered with blood. We then rolled James' body over. A large cross was tattooed on his back covered with blood. Beside it were the words: "Only God can Judge Me."

I prayed the words of Jesus, "Don't judge and you will not be judged. Don't condemn and you will not be condemned. Forgive and you will be forgiven. Give and it will be given, a good measure pressed down and shaken together and overflowing into your lap. The measure with which you measure will be measured back to you."

Since James didn't seem to judge or condemn, I forgave his sins. Since James gave his life, God gave it back and then some. "Jesus, remember me when you come into your Kingdom." God bless you, James, for "Today, you will be with me in Paradise."*

"Forgive them; they know not what they do."

I left briefly and returned to pray with the brothers. I offered up the last of the seven of them and the third who had died. Eric had very little blood or wounds. He was Baptist. *"Thanks and praise for our days, 'neath the sun, 'neath the stars, 'neath the sky. As we go, this we know, God is 'nigh."* Then I sang "Amazing Grace" as the Marines of Mortuary Affairs prayed with us. Sweetly, gently, and incredibly, Jesus welcomed Eric home.

And that is my story. Raleigh, Eric and James left their bodies behind. They joined our loving God. Faith comforted and encouraged me.

God may not always be obvious, but He is there: discernible,
knowable, reachable, dependable,
and ever welcoming.
– Author Unknown

One day we will join our brothers if we simply turn our lives over to Jesus, the one who was crucified and died and rose again. For the living, like Philip, Eddie, Quincy, Brandon and me, part of us has died. We will never again be wholly of this world. Yet, we were resurrected from this very dark night of our souls.

We must unlock the door that guards our grief when loved ones die. We must then cross the threshold to share the peace we know in Christ Jesus. Jesus said, "Peace be with you." We must expose our wounds and the sting of death, not in vengeance, but in grace and mercy for all. O my Jesus, forgive us our sins. Save us from the fires of hell. Lead all souls to heaven, especially those who most need your mercy.

The wounds of grief and death are deep and real. Share them, and rejoice as Jesus did with his disciples, mother and friends. *"As the Father has sent me, so I send you." And then he breathed on them. "Receive the Holy Spirit. If you forgive each other's sins, they will be forgiven. If you hold them bound, they are held bound."*

Is there a person in your life who binds you? Do you need to forgive someone? The only gift God desires from his children is for us to love and forgive one another for all eternity. We must step out in faith, for we have received Jesus, the one who continually forgives.

Philip did return to his platoon but was eventually sent back to the U.S. His wounds were not healing properly. Before Philip's departure, I had the opportunity to pray with him and share this story. He signed my journal:

God Bless you, Sir & Thank You

Philip S. Levine

* Some months later, I was asked to pray at a Marine Corps Reunion in Jacksonville, Florida. A veteran of the Marines approached me and inquired about James Phillips, the deceased Marine with the large cross tattoo on his back. The Vietnam veteran had escorted James' body at his funeral in Plant City, Florida.

I retrieved my green journal and flipped straight to my entry about James. James had been the only son of Lisa, his mother. I will never forget the day she called me a few weeks later. Her call came while I was driving on the ramp from I-95 to I-295. When I offered James up to God, I had never envisioned his mother and father would later become my friends. Our God is an Awesome God!

From an electronic letter:

Father Ron, how are you? I am on page 234 of your book. You did a good job on the book. Thank you for writing about James, that means a lot. You were right when you said James and God brought us together and for us to be friends. It was meant for me to find you. God bless you, Ron, and thank you for praying over my son James, it was meant for you to be there. I know James thanks you, too.

Lisa Phillips (22 May 2008)

\+ James R. Phillips + Raleigh C. Smith +Eric Hillenburg

Chapter X

CHRISTMAS IN FALLUJAH

On Christmas Eve, I traveled to six different units in Fallujah to celebrate Mass. At 9:00 p.m., we headed back to camp, but there was an accident with one of the Humvees in our convoy. I was asked to exit the Humvee. Patrick and I stood just outside Fallujah, along the main road. Nothing but stars and sand were visible. Rain soon appeared which quickly turned to mud. The air was bitterly cold. After approximately an hour, we were picked up and taken to Camp Fallujah. Thank God! I arrived at 11:30 p.m., barely in time to celebrate midnight Mass with over three-hundred people. On Christmas Day, I celebrated Mass and Communion services at different companies all day and afternoon.

My last Mass of the day was at the command post in Fallujah. I celebrated my nineteenth service of Christmas with about twenty servicemen. Afterward, I ate dinner in a small room and Dominic, a lance corporal, asked me to sit with him. A Navy corpsman was also present, and I offered him my last St. Christopher medal, which was hanging around my neck. He eagerly accepted the medal. I then inquired as to his denomination. He laughed as he replied, "Jewish. And you can't have your medal back!"

Dominic hadn't been able to receive Communion since he'd been on watch. I told him I had the Eucharist with me. Conscious of the church rules regarding reception of the Body of Christ, Dominic replied, “But I just ate!” I assured him in extreme situations, church rules could be waived. Dominic joyfully received Communion at that moment. “Come to the table!” said the Lord. Immediately after Dominic received the Eucharist, “O Holy Night” played over the speaker system. We all toasted with our non-alcoholic wine.

After dinner, I began walking out of the command post. A sergeant tapped my shoulder and said one man on lookout hoped to receive Communion. I was completely exhausted, and the thought of climbing five flights of stairs was overwhelming.

“Let’s go!” I said.

As I ascended the top floor of the command post, I smelled rotten odors and commented to the accompanying sergeant. It could have been spoiled food or dead animals or people… I saw four men there and asked which one was Catholic. A young kid, nineteen at most, was smoking and came forward. He wanted Communion. I told him he might need to put the cigarette out first. After he did so, we walked to a cold, filthy, empty room to celebrate the Eucharist. As I proclaimed the Gospel, the young man appeared angelic, as if this could be his last chance to hear it. Of course, he thought my idea was crazy that it was to be the best Christmas ever.

I gave him Communion, putting the Body of Christ in his stained, battle-scarred hands. I thought of Mary, the Mother of Jesus, wrapping her newborn baby in swaddling clothes and laying him in a manger because there had been no room for him in this cold world. I then began singing "O Holy Night." The two of us, a Marine Private and a Navy Chaplain, bellowed out the song for all of Fallujah and the whole world to hear. At the end of the song, we laughed in joy! The tears streamed down our faces. He looked at me and said, "Padre, this ***is*** the best Christmas ever." And I knew I had received the best Christmas gift of my life, the privilege of being there in Iraq. God is Good!

Young Corpsman and her niece
(August 2, 2004)
The day we left for Iraq

Christmas in the City of Fallujah
with RP3 Demetri Givans beside me

Chapter XI

TEARS in the DESERT

January and February 2005

6 January 2005 — After the Battle for Fallujah

Bravo Surgical has had no casualties for days. Peace is boring in a combat zone, especially on a deployment. We have been in Iraq for four months. The days have been mostly intense; there has been precious little time for reflection. Now I have time, and I am bored and mildly depressed. I still have much to do with ministry, but so many of us at Bravo Surgical Company have thoughts and feelings bottled up which preserve the fragility of our psyches.

So what am I protecting?

I won't get into that. I am bored now that I am deprived and empty of casualties and 'angels.' My thoughts sicken me. Should I be ashamed?

My adrenaline is low. I had wearied of keeping up the pace, yet now I miss the excitement. I miss the affirmation. I need to go home. Is this what soldiers and Marines experience after leaving the front lines of battle and conflict? Could this be why so many stay in the military and remain soldiers?

O the adjustment, the processing yet to do. The chaplains sponsor a "Warrior Transition Brief." Does it make a difference? As a chaplain, I seriously doubt it. Of course, I sound negative. I have gone from experiencing daily torments and shredding of bodies to relative peace in my world, although I remain in a combat zone. What's wrong with that?

I am bored.

I'm not even shocked by my thoughts anymore.

Something in me cries for healing.

I cry for peace.

Here it is, a peaceful state, and I can take it or leave it.

Do I take pain and suffering and death for granted?

Where is God?

War has tainted me, even though I tried to do good and avoid evil. Yet, my thoughts are ugly and shameful. Have mercy on my soul. How will I survive? How will we survive?

Heal my soul, Beloved. Allow me to enjoy this peace even if it is boring. Help me to long for it again when I am thrust into the jaws, the horror and the traps of war!!!

6 February 2005 — Confirmation

Since September, I have been preparing twenty-four service members for full Initiation into the Catholic Church. We met on Tuesday evenings, and I also held make-up sessions. The compressed classes were very taxing and demanding. In the desert, there was some time to reflect and process information, even though we were exceptionally busy.

Of this group, six had already been baptized in another Christian faith. They needed to be received into the Church and then confirmed in the Spirit before receiving First Eucharist (Communion). Confirmation is similar to Jesus' baptism in the Jordan. When he emerged from the water, a voice from heaven said, "This is my beloved son with whom I am well pleased!"

One of the men had been injured the night before, so we received him into the Church and confirmed him that evening at Bravo Surgical. He took "Israel" for his Confirmation name. How appropriate, for Israel means "to wrestle with God."

Celebrating Mass at a flour factory in Fallujah (Dec 2004)

The Memorial Service

(January 20, 2005)

Seven rifles,

Seven helmets,

Seven dog tags,

Seven pairs of boots,

A river of tears, yet no sobbing.

Seven men no longer recognizable,

Yet intensely felt in their absence.

Empty and yet full of emotions and spirit.

Lima Company

Third Battalion

First Marines

Battle of Fallujah

Stars and Stripes

Semper Fidelis

Always Faithful

Marine Corps Flag

Eagle, globe and anchor – red & gold

My soul is weeping along with my body

Lamentations of the soul

A time to reflect

An invocation:

A call to God

A cry, a plea

A moment of expectation…

To welcome the True One of Honor

into our grief, sorrow, hopes, expectations…

and emptiness

Amazing Grace

Gift of the Presence of God

Of Life

Of honor and respect of soul

Reflections on life lived with gratitude and imperfection.

And somehow, I must proclaim the Benediction.

Roll Call

Seven missing yet intensely felt

Taps

Passing on the Torch of Compassion

We can only hope to give the best care possible to our heroes and heroines.

When medicine has gone to its limits
Or sometimes even beyond
In the compassionate care of the providers
It is then that the
Spiritual dimension of the human person
Shifts into high gear

It was already there, this spiritual dimension
Even in her denial
But at the moment of pain that escapes
the morphine
and encouraging words
and even tears of the soul…

That is when your RMT
Religious Ministry Team
facilitates the
Faith or lack thereof…

Within the indomitable

mysterious

wholly incredible

person

human being

and spirit

To save

That source and summit

Beyond death

And yet below, that is attainable

As I have witnessed

And borne with gratitude and trepidation

When a son or daughter of our nation is close to breathing no more,

Or even after the breath has been stolen away,

It is then that we ask their final wish and receive their final statement

In the timeless moment before departure

stripped of all earthly desire

life runs dry

A chaplain records and witnesses this miracle of death

And the RMT can teach the Medical Team to provide likewise

Let us journey with great love, hope, and humility.
Let us celebrate the hours and days and minutes that will transform
and transfigure our wounded, dead, and their families forever!

AMEN.

We can only imagine
what our kind acts, our compassion, our love, and our skills will
create in eternity.
We can only imagine.

Chaplain Ron Moses Camarda +
Camp Fallujah, Iraq
February 24, 2005

Chapter XII

Journey out of the Desert

(EXODUS)

1 March 2005

Camp Fallujah

During our last week in Fallujah, Tim, our dentist, visited me in my office (a converted bathroom).

We shared.

We prayed.

Tim wasn't Catholic but had been a strong, faithful Christian his entire life. He had played his guitar at Midnight Mass. Although gifted with my father's voice, I had greatly appreciated his accompaniment on guitar. We needed Tim there. The Christmas decorations were a bit tacky in a room once occupied by Saddam Hussein and his henchmen. We had used glowsticks of red and green to make a cross. Nevertheless, I had been taken aback by how special and meaningful the simple beauty was for us at that particular time. The horrific battle had ended, and we were changed forever. We needed a Holy Night with a thrill of hope for a weary world.

We sang "O Holy Night."

The music was beyond beautiful. It resonated within our souls.

Would God have called us all the way into the desert to play and sing this song on midnight at Christmas?

Yes. Yes, it was possible.

Another tear in the desert.

The Marines of Mortuary Affairs "enjoying" my Combat Transition Brief.

6 March 2005 — TQ Camp, Iraq

We flew out of Camp Fallujah aboard helicopters. We were the second and last wave to leave at this time. Our exit was rather peaceful. I couldn't believe we were actually returning home. I rarely, if ever, allowed myself to anticipate this day.

As I sit in a tent at TQ Camp, I reflect on my experiences. It is Sunday. Last night I celebrated my last Mass in Iraq, the Saturday vigil at Camp Fallujah. The relief priest had arrived and would be taking over. It was time for me to return. This morning, with not much to do, I attended Mass and was very emotional. Tears streamed from my eyes. I must begin the long journey out of the desert and then home. It will take more than a couple of weeks to make it back to Jacksonville. It won't be easy.

However, I am at home in the desert, for the Lord of All has found me…

I love you Jesus. You know my heart!

7 March 2005 — Joy in the Journey (Sort of)

Joy in the journey

We are on our way

But it is difficult

To avoid looking ahead to our reunion

With friends and family

Jesus, my friend, my beloved,

Thank you for your love, forgiveness, and grace

Breathe on us.

Purify us.

Inspire us.

A tent with 49 other sailors and Marines

Language isn't as bad as Marines alone

But it is atrocious,

Everything they say, everything they listen to

And force the rest of us to hear

Is laced with expletives and sometimes sayings like,

"I swear to God"

And I wonder if God is a thought

Who knows? What I do know is that

My time with them is coming to an end

And I am not sure I want it to be forever.

This is a crazy world in which we live.

Somehow I ended up in the middle of this tent

Saturday night cold as hell

Sunday night a fit sleep, with earplugs

Monday night we begin to get on each other's nerves

We have Tuesday and Wednesday still to go

Thursday we fly out

Then we have Thursday and Friday

at Camp Victory in Kuwait

And then the long flight home.

Love and gratitude still

Much to reflect, ponder, and write

But now it is time to sleep.

Love, Joy, Peace, and Hope!

8 March 2005 — Be Glad!

Be glad!

Waiting to fly home

Yet this is a special time

Jesus flows through me…fast…and yet slow

My soul is soaring in love

It is hard to imagine that I am on my way out of the desert

Yet, I will forever be in the desert

And, of course, that is fine with me because Jesus,

my friend and beloved,

is there

is here

forever

drawing me closer to his heart

Jesus amazes me and thrills me

Life without God is nothing; it is rubbish

God always and in all ways, since I was in my mother's womb

And probably before that

Is thrilled with me!?!

God, my father, loves me

With great passion and compassion

Revealed in Jesus

Touched by his Spirit

9 March 2005

We live in very stark conditions. There is nothing to do as we await transportation. The main part of camp is a bus ride away. I gladly take the 20-30 minute trip so I don't have to use the portable toilets or take a shower here in this separated part of camp. It is difficult to pray at this time.

10 March 2005 **Torrential Downpour in the Desert**

Last Day in Iraq

Now this was a day I wish to forget.

I awoke on a cot in a tent with fifty others. I began praying the Office of Readings but then met with Sergeant Mark Ard, the oldest of seven brothers. We ate breakfast together after taking a bus to the main camp about two miles down a dusty, littered road. We spoke, shared, and visited the chapel for healing and prayer. Heal him, Jesus. We then reflected on the last seven statements of Jesus before died; yesterday, I had written the words on a dry erase board in the chapel. "Today you will be with me in paradise." We slowly prayed Psalms 22, 23 and 139. Blessed be God who heals us in Christ. Heal him, Lord. Heal Mark. Thank you.

I stopped by the rustic weight room in a tent and pushed my muscles. The exercise was therapeutic. After waiting for the bus and sitting in it, I finally finished the Office of Readings.

The skies looked very gray and heavily laden with rain. My last day in the desert would now include unforgettable torrential rains. We stood outside waiting for customs inspection with all of our gear. The skies opened up, and all of us were soaked to the bones. When I finally entered the customs tent with my duffle bags, I realized the rain had drenched my bags completely. Our wet bags would now be packed in wetness for 72 hours. Things would be ruined. Mold would form. And another smell would be added to our memories of the desert. Only this time we would bring the smells home! The unusual rain followed us to Kuwait. We watched our pallet of gear soak up the rain and get tremendously wet.

But we are going home! We won't see those bags until arriving on the grinder at Camp Pendleton, California. The joy upon greeting our families and loved ones will overpower the smell. After the gear check-in ordeal, we returned to our tent and it was now raining both inside and out. My cot happened to be in the center of the tent so I enjoyed a small, dry spot before the waters eventually encircled me then soaked my cot and those of my brothers and sisters. The situation was very depressing.

As we waited for nightfall in order to depart Iraq, the next seven or eight hours were miserable. However, I was reading an interesting book by Anthony Destefano that my sister had given me about Heaven. I also listened to music by John Michael Talbot on my CD player. I felt suspended both in the tent and then in the hangar. Tears and love flowed out of me like a river. No one saw this. I wasn't sobbing, but something was clearly happening within me. Was I being cleansed?

We left Iraq just minutes before midnight. The flight felt like Mr. Toad's Wild Ride. Our waterlogged luggage and gear was with us in the C-130. I couldn't believe we were actually leaving Iraq until that heavy plane was airborne. Within minutes, however, I was airsick. I had the dry heaves. I was lucky, though. Many actually threw up.

12 March 2005 — Camp Victory, Kuwait

We were heading home, but countless people would not truly return as they left it. Many people were severely and physically injured. Many more were mentally and spiritually wounded. My family and friends were affected positively because I was coming home alive and basically unscathed. I hope this will be the case in the months and years to come. I must wait and see.

We arrived to more rain and even windstorms.

In this camp, there were lines for everything. However, there was a great sense of joy, expectation and relief. Even though there was absolutely no privacy, I retreated into a very solitary and lonely space within myself. I attended Mass both days at the chapel. I disappeared into the company and did not socialize with others. I rarely talked. I yearned to escape from everyone. In some ways, it was worse than indoctrination at the Merchant Marine

Academy. Some of the leadership wanted to micro-manage others. My understanding is similar to when I don't want to work on myself, I try to manage others. I am not always willing to work on my own sense of self.

Inching up to the commercial plane was a nightmare. It was like being trapped in snarled traffic and that if only the traffic lights were synchronized, the traffic would flow. The buses didn't know where to go. There were numerous delays. Anxieties were very high. The experience would have been a debacle had we not eventually boarded the plane. The whole ordeal tested our patience. Late that night, after numerous delays, I was finally seated on the plane.

13 March 2005 — In the Air

Flying away from the desert, my surroundings feel almost surreal. I am thousands of feet in the sky traveling over five-hundred miles per hour to reach home. Where is home?

I am different than when I arrived in Iraq over six months ago. I love God deeply, who is my Beloved. My soul thirsts for more. I never want to return to the place I was before going into the desert. I have much to ponder, much to reflect, and there is time.

Somehow, I was placed in first class on this flight. I am not cramped. I am pleasantly at peace. Maybe I have already shed most of my tears, but maybe I have not. My Father sent me on a mission. People say I am a hero. I would like to believe this, but I know better. I was simply placed in Fallujah to be Christ for the poor in spirit. God sent me for a short time, although it often felt as if it was never ending. Jesus never abandoned me. Jesus shared a dimension and depth of love with me that was sometimes overwhelming.

God has blessed me with many gifts in my life. These gifts were all used during the past six months. When I was utterly spent, Jesus made me even more effective. The Holy Spirit is truly a friend and companion to me. What could I possibly fear? As it has been all my life, if I allow a "fear" of anything to influence my discernment and any choices, Jesus gently but firmly helps me confront and defeat that fear.

I had always feared the Middle East. It terrorized and paralyzed me. That is where God sent me when I thought I had "dodged the bullet." God sent me to the heart of the war. Not only did I receive the angels (KIA) and wounded, but I was pushed into the heart of a city which harbored incredible evil. God sent me into the broken and shredded hearts of our young and embattled Marines, sailors and soldiers.

How reluctant could I be?

True to my name, Ron Moses, I hemmed and hawed and made excuses to avoid confronting my fears. I criticized my brothers. I even begged God to send someone else. I so admired the other chaplains who went before me into that city of hatred, Fallujah.

Yet, I realized innocent children live in Fallujah. Parents who love their children live there, too. Children of God live there. How could I have said no? Yet, I tried my best to say no time and time again. I am ashamed to admit this.

I have truly been the son who says, "NO!" But I hope I then responded with a love that barely supersedes my fears.

Ron Moses traveled into the desert of the Middle East, into the desert of his heart, and finally into the desert of his soul. I do know how to do this. God has been training me since my youth to "go into Egypt and rescue his people from slavery." However, the people to whom I was sent did not know they were enslaved. The people to whom I am still sent do not realize it, either.

I love you I Am!

I love you Beloved!

I love you Father!

I love you Jesus!

I love you Holy Spirit!

My Guardian Angel protected me during all my journeys. My angel has a name, Patrick Moses +. Thank you, Patrick Moses, for your protection and love. I love you! Sorry I haven't told you sooner. Well done! Well done! But we aren't done yet, and I am sure you know that already! Let us make our Creator proud! Let's have some fun!

Dear Jesus,

After living in the desert for over six months during the Battle for Fallujah, I am flying to California. It is March 13, even where I am headed. I am between countries, missions, and pastor assignments. God has set my course, and I am not anxious or even upset about my future. Discernment seems out of my reach.

So Jesus, my Beloved friend, I love you. Wherever you send me, I will go as long as you convey your desire and your will for me.

Save us, Jesus.

Lead us to your light.

Amen!

A Letter from Saint James (4:1-10):

Beloved: Where do the wars and where do the conflicts among you come from? Is it not from your passions that make war within your members? You covet but do not possess. You kill and envy but you cannot ask. You ask but do not receive, because you ask wrongly, to spend it on your passions....So submit yourselves to God. Resist the Devil, and he will flee from you. Draw near to God, and he will draw near to you...

Still Flying on 13 March 2005

O Jesus

I am so wounded,

O my soul is so tired

I don't know how to rest

To take a day and enjoy doing nothing

For seven months,

I have been for others, spiritually and physically

But me?

I am shredded, bludgeoned, and isolated

Help me, Lord,

Heal my weary and torn heart

The Landing Prayer

The flight was incredibly comfortable. I would have loved a glass of wine with my meals, though! An hour before landing, the flight attendants learned I was a chaplain and asked me to say a prayer over the intercom. A truly joyous feeling permeated the airplane. All of us wanted to return home and get on with our lives, yet our lives would never be the same. We would never think about things in quite the same way. Almost all of us experienced a physical or emotional death. Our inner wounds were not visible to others. Many of us might even deny our need for inner healing.

I prepared a prayer in my heart and scribbled a few notes in my ragged green journal. Its pages were no longer new, crisp and innocent. I first noticed a page with the third verse of the "Star Spangled Banner" written on it. I then wrote, as best as I could remember, the words to "America the Beautiful." We had just crossed into our home country, and it was a beautiful morning. We felt the purple mountains in all their majesty.

I began my prayer by asking the men and women in the very large plane to breathe in…and then breathe out…

And then I sang:

O Beautiful for spacious skies
For amber waves of grain
For purple mountains majesty
Above the fruited plane
America, America
God shed his grace on thee
And crown thy good with brotherhood
From sea to shining sea

Let us remember our beloved brothers and sisters who died while serving the country we love. Thanks to you all who serve and thanks to God for our families whom we couldn't do this without.

Oh, thus be it ever when free men shall stand,

Between their loved homes and the war's desolation;

Blest with vict'ry and peace,

May the heav'n-rescued land

Praise the Power that has made

and preserved us a nation.

Then conquer we must, when our cause it is just,

And this be our motto: "In God is our trust;"

And the Star-Spangled Banner in triumph shall wave

O'er the land of the free and the home of the brave.

Amen!

13 March 2006 — Arriving Home?

Families and friends would excitedly greet the majority of those getting off the plane this day. Patrick's wife and children drove out from Ohio to greet him. Since I was from the East Coast and a Naval Reservist, my homecoming would be somewhat hollow. However, my very dear and intimate friends, the Kearney's, had driven from Las Vegas to both greet me and take me to their home for the requisite "96" hours. These were four free days given to help servicemembers readjust before returning to the company for work, or in my case, to begin the process of demobilization.

After landing at March Air Field, we underwent a long process and ended up at Camp Pendleton's parade field. We stayed in the hangar for a very long time. I was frustrated, and I wanted to escape this company. We were truly getting on each other's nerves. People often try to make their reunion perfect which is an unrealistic fantasy. After being separated from loved ones for over six months, an adjustment period will be necessary. As a chaplain, I always encouraged people to "take it easy" when returning from deployment. I had been away on many missions, but I had never been with a group of sailors or Marines returning from deployment. My homecomings had never been a big deal. However, I had never returned from a war.

The sailors and Marines turned in their firearms to the armory. Although I had no weapon, I was with them until the bitter end. As we pulled into the reception area, my heart started pounding. I desperately wanted to hug someone I knew and loved. John and Nancy Kearney had worked beside me from 1997-2000 after my last active duty assignment. They are dear friends and the parents of five sons; the two youngest want to become Marines. Matt and Kyle were both in high school at that time and called me 'Uncle.' It was truly wonderful to finally get off the bus.

John, Nancy, and the boys helped me unpack some of my wet bags. The smell was atrocious. I kept just a few things with me, and we drove to Las Vegas. It was truly grand. I would fly to San Diego on March 17, St. Patrick's Day. Then, I would rent a car and drive to Prince of Peace Benedictine Monastery in Oceanside, just south of Camp Pendleton. I would stay at the monastery while I began the demobilization process. There was just one hitch.

Nancy was actively involved with the Marine Corps League. Her family had been incredibly supportive of the Marines in Iraq. One of the local Marines, John Lukac, died in Fallujah and had been received by me. John's parents were emotionally distraught over the loss of their son, and Nancy thought it would be comforting if I could meet with them. I had to contemplate this. I was more tired and drained than I had previously realized. In a way, meeting a deceased soldier's family would be more painful than serving in Iraq.

I slept a lot while at John and Nancy's home. I am not a gambler, so I didn't care about visiting the Vegas Strip, but we did go look around. Finally, I agreed to meet Helena and Jan Lukac and their other son, Peter. This visit was a tremendous blessing for John's parents, brother, and me. I wrote the following in my journal:

John Lukac +, Son of Jan & Helen, Brother of Peter

Last night, we prayed. Nancy and I prayed that the Spirit of Jesus would guide us in finding words of comfort for the Lukac family. Matthew and Kyle, the youngest sons of Nancy and John, journeyed with us into this valley of tears.

John Lukac was born on April 20, 1985, and died suddenly on October 30, 2004, in Fallujah, Iraq. I was the chaplain who received his body. God placed me there, so I could be here at this time. John was so young, like the beloved disciple. When Saint John stood beneath the bloody cross, his life changed forever. Jesus, who could barely speak, gave John his own mother. The mother was given another son, as Jesus knew he would die. Yet, his Father raised Jesus from the dead.

Something very special happened as I waited at length for the bodies to arrive from this horrific blast. When the bodies finally came, and John's fellow Marines identified them, I begged God for help. "Help me, God, to make sense of such tragedy. These were just boys who had barely even left their parents' homes."

John Lukac died over four months ago. I found myself at his home in Las Vegas with his grieving parents and younger brother. His mom and dad were from Hungary and Czechoslovakia. They had escaped oppression and communism and immigrated to the United States in 1983. Now they were oppressed by grief. Their oldest son was sacrificed by this great nation. I am not sure our country realizes the sacrifice this family has offered for us. They reluctantly offered their son in order to preserve peace and a way of life that isn't always filled with love, honor, respect, decency *and selflessness. Part of me believes war is often about money. Somehow, we can't even question this possibility.*

How do John's death and sacrifice, and Jan and Helena's devastation make us better persons, better citizens, and more generous souls? John was only nineteen years old.

I am a priest. All four members of this family were baptized Catholic. For years, Jan and Helena were not free to worship God. Sometimes, to worship brought certain death. As a result, Dad loves this country. John knew his dad loved this country. This gratitude most certainly weighed on John's decision to honor his father and enter the Marine Corps of the United States.

As we wept and looked through the pictures of John's funeral, Jan shared that the Marines are like family, brothers forever. When one dies, the others take it so personally, for their brother and best friend has died. No one is left behind. That is what made the whole nightmare of that night even worse. The bodies arrived in an almost unrecognizable state, but they were returned. I was awed and humbled when John's brother Marines identified his broken and charred remains. I had no doubt they knew who was whom. And so, at the time, I prayed in a fog…

However, I remember the agonizing evening in crystal clear details; the memories are more than my heart or mind can possibly acknowledge or endure. I do not just remember; I am transported to that truly awful, dark night. And yet, being present on that evening was necessary so I could now be here with Helena and Jan, still stuck in the desert where their son returned to the dust as we will all do some day.

I walked with the Marines who brought in the dead on that dark and sad evening. I pierced the demonic darkness and forced my body and soul to recover beyond their shock and terror so that Jesus within me could touch and begin to heal. I also desperately thirsted for this healing.

It seems impossible to overcome these diabolical and horrendous wounds to our spirits and souls. O Beloved God, how did you know to send Nancy, her sons and me to the home of Jan and Helena Lukac and their son Peter? You do hear our prayer. This family is so poor today. Before, I thought the dying soldier was the poorest person in the world. The parents are also the poorest except the pain is worse. The parents still breathe and must face this catastrophe every day for the rest of their lives. This holds true for spouses, children and families of those who perish from war.

I loved the men and women who were killed or severely wounded. Am I also poor? Blessed are the poor in spirit, for theirs is the Kingdom of God. Blessed are they who mourn, for they shall be comforted. So here I am again, groping for words, groping for something to share. I reluctantly experience death all over again.

Blessed are you when they insult you and persecute you and utter every kind of slander against you because of me. Rejoice and be glad, for great will be your reward in Heaven.

John Lukac +

Courageous

Loving

"Little Mommy Great Kisser"

Good

Smart

Hilarious

Brave

Sense of Humor

Honest

Careful

Thoughtful

Endurance

Strength

Compassion

Respectful

Enjoyed good food

Loved family

Helena cooked a wonderful meal, and we prayed together with great love. The family shared the preceding words to describe their son and brother. I was honored to be there with them.

The program and card from the funeral of John Lukac

18 March 2005 — Prince of Peace Abbey

Evening

I fasted all day and intended to continue all night, but the good brother monks invited me to dine with them in silence…

It was delicious.

Father Sharbel said I looked as if I had lost some weight since last August. And so I have. Without further thought, I took two helpings.

19 March 2005

Good morning, Beloved!

I love you. It is early morning, many blessings. It is the Feast of St. Joseph, husband of Mary, Queen of the Universe. You, O Lord, are a gentle teacher. You take my hand and lead me where I do not want to go in the flesh, yet I desire with all my being…Wow!

Dinner with the Monks

Father Herbert, age 91

Father Abbot, age 96

Brother Philip

Brother Paul

Brother Benedict told me in Iraq, "Your room is waiting"

Father Sharbel

Brother Mario

So many wonderful Monks

A joy, companionship, a home!

21 March 2005 **Passion Sunday**

God here present with me, before the Tabernacle

Holy of Holies

Feeling sorry for myself

Exhausted yet healthy

I try to exercise more so that I can eat more

I am trying to escape my passions and the work I must do

and long to do

Here I am

I come to do Your will

And yet, I have nothing

I am nothing,

Empty

Alone

Shattered

You, Alone, O Lord, can heal me

You, Alone

Body and Blood of I AM

Inebriate Me!

Now!

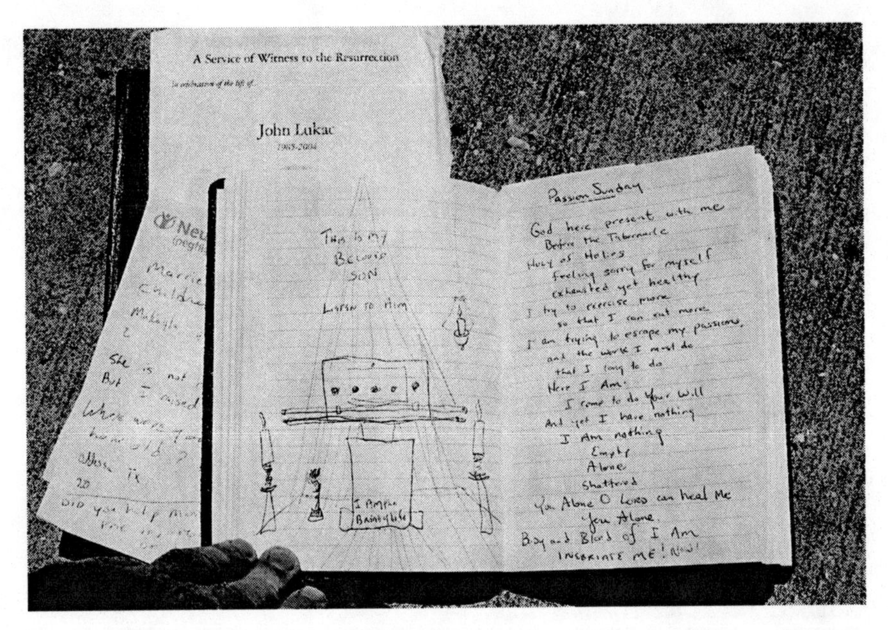

I am not an artist, but I drew the tabernacle at Prince of Peace Abbey on Passion Sunday in March of 2005.

(Prescription notepad from dialogue with Christopher in "Speechless," p. 192)

22 March 2005 — Tuesday of Holy Week

The Journey continues home.

I am always trying to control, feel comfortable.

My outburst of irritation and ire today was not appropriate, was not gentle,

and was not of You O Lord.

Here you are, calling me home and I am like a wild dog chasing my tail while the enemy pursues me.

Help me, Lord to be like you.

I am so afraid to be alone.

Good morning, I love you.

Vigils

Alone

Cool Morning Air

Almost cold, but not quite

Restless and peaceful

Both at the same time

Jesus

You love me

I do love You, Lord

No matter where I go, even into the dark void of my soul,

You will not let me go alone

Even alone, I AM is with Me.

Walk quick swift into your arms

And me, wee me

Desires to have You, O Beloved

Rest in my arms, my embrace

O my.

22 & 24 March 2005 — The Long Flight Home

Unholy Week

I checked out of the unit in less than two days. It was a whirlwind. I ended up on the road and away from Community for the Easter Triduum. Thankfully, I managed to secure a ticket through Military Personnel for Tuesday night, the "Red Eye." I would first go through Jacksonville, North Carolina, in order to demobilize at Camp Lejeune. I had hoped to be home by Thursday evening for the Last Supper in Jacksonville, Florida. I wish someone had coached me to "Breathe in…Breathe out…"

My duty is done, except to travel the last flights home. I will fly from San Diego to Los Angeles to Charlotte to Jacksonville, NC, and eventually to Jacksonville, FL. Maybe I'll arrive home by Good Friday!

Through the Desert God led his people

God's love endures forever.

Psalm 136:16

Let us therefore, learn to pass from one imperfect activity to another without worrying too much about what we are missing. It is true that we make many mistakes. But the biggest of them is to be surprised at them: as if we had some hope of never making any.

Music is pleasing not only because of the sound but because of the silence that is in it: Without alternation of sound and silence there would be no rhythm. If we strive to be happy by filling all the silences of life with sound, productive by turning all life's leisure into work, and real by turning all our being into doing, we will only succeed in producing a <u>*hell*</u> *on earth.*

– Thomas Merton

Last Leg of the Journey Home

It is almost anticlimactic

I am finally going home.

My home is in Atlantic Beach, Florida

I miss my home

My friends, my family,

I can't believe I can rest for awhile.

So much has happened, so much.

I will be home for the Supper!!!

I am Thrilled!

What a journey this has been.

So much to ponder

So much to reflect

Bill, a retired Marine Master Gunnery Sergeant from Vietnam, got this airline ticket for me, the only possible way home

God bless him!

It will take more than a lifetime to make sense of my experience in Iraq. The time was remarkable, breathtaking, heart-wrenching, and thrilling. It was also frightening, sorrowful, and traumatic.

So often, I had to arrest my anxieties which yanked at me like a herd of wild horses. I was constantly lured and tortured by the temptation to live in the future rather than in the moment. God was with me, however. When I waited patiently and sank deep into the moments, dry as they mostly were, God's defined and steady love rained on me in the desert.

I, Ron Moses, traveled into the desert after specifically saying, "No, I won't go!" I am filled with gratitude. I am changed forever. I will continue to blunder and make mistakes, and I learned that. I have often criticized others for not acknowledging their mistakes, when I, too, am one who hides. I "blow it" on a daily basis. Maybe I will learn to hide less. I am still being perfected by God.

I cherish the tears

The inconveniences

The disgusting smells of death

The sorrow, the gut-wrenching fear

The boredom

The excitement

The fame

I honor the life given to me.

I honor the lives entrusted to me.

I believe that God called me into the Desert

And God, ALONE

Sure, I didn't know this at first

But now, I realize who else could have?

All is Beauty

For All is God's

Created, Celebrated, and Raised!

Lord of Life

Lord of the Dance

Thank You, O Beloved Jesus

Thank You

It is You, I AM

In love with me?

What could I possibly fear?

God Alone!!!

Home alone, at last!

12 April 2005 Atlantic Beach, Florida

We walk by faith, not by sight. -2 Corinthians 5:7

Yes, we walk by faith, not by sight.

I am at home in Atlantic Beach, Florida. My work with the Navy is complete, but my work also seems to be beginning. It is April 12, and I signed my DD214 (formal record of active duty time) on April 2. I am on terminal leave for six more days. Technically, I remain on active duty until that time, but I have essentially been released from the Navy. Yet, my real work has only just begun. Almost nine months ago, I left Saint Patrick's as their pastor and went to Iraq. My departure was a whirlwind. Truly, I didn't know if I would return. I am grateful for my life.

Many didn't return home. Some might have lived their lives differently had they known the outcome. Over 81 human beings died before me. Over 1,500 were wounded physically. How many tens of thousands were permanently affected by shrapnel to their souls? The statistics are staggering. This war could eventually be more damaging than the Vietnam War when truths are revealed.

Great work is needed to sort the thoughts and movements of my heart. My intent is not to assign blame but to reflect on what drives our hearts to make certain choices. As children of God, we must ponder whether we use our God-given gifts for good or evil. It is both our honor and duty to choose goodness. Are we driven by carnal desires? Or do we learn to make wise choices blended with understanding, appropriate judgments, compassion and knowledge? Are we courageous enough to resist the Evil One? Are we humble enough to worship and express gratitude through our reverence for the Truly Holy Creative Force of Love? Do we dance in the Light of the Divine? Do we wonder and stand in awe of the magnificence of life?

During my time in Iraq, one particular casualty was a suicide. Pablito arrived with an unexploded bomb in the belly of his soul. He wasn't physically breathing, but I saw and felt his breath and life before me. Pablito's life was precious. God held this man before me. Jesus wept and begged me to help him.

Jesus held his beloved child and asked me to restore him to life.

I complained. I cried to Jesus in the silence of my heart, "How can I do such a thing? I have no faith! I am so wounded myself!" And Jesus pierced my heart and said, "You do have faith because I give it to you! I am not holding Pablito. I hold you in my arms! Arise!"

Jesus reminds me, "Do not be afraid."
"Peace be with you."
Jesus shows me his wounds.
"Peace be with you."
"As the Father has sent me, so I send you."
Jesus breathed on me.
Jesus anointed me.
Jesus washed my feet.

I received the Holy Spirit.

I was commanded to forgive the sins of Pablito.

I was commanded to forgive your sins.

...and I must forgive myself.

I bent over and kissed my little brother, Pablito. Although very few will acknowledge his heroic life, God does. The truth is that God loves Pablito. God has the final Word. God returns his life to him. God promised.

Part of our failure to address the tragedy of suicide is because of Judas. Judas betrayed Jesus and then ended his own life in despair. We inadvertently associate the act of suicide with betrayal of Jesus, and we should not. Suicide devastates the loved ones of the deceased person, but the greater problem lies in our refusal to recognize the flame of Christ in each of us. Because of our attachment to the physical world, we fail to see eternal life revealed by God through his Son, Jesus and the Holy Spirit.

As I write this book months after my return, I am frustrated by my inability to remember every detail of those people who came to me, especially all of the individuals who died. Details could help comfort and heal many families. Hopefully, those who either lost loved ones in this war or left parts of their own bodies or blood in Iraq will be consoled by hearing my story.

After my friend, Jon, committed suicide in 1982, his mother tried to unlock the "mystery" of it for many years. Where was Jon? Who had he encountered? Why at that time? I never told her she needed to get over it, because that would have been cruel and insensitive. I usually listened for awhile and then shared my own love of her son, our experiences, and my hope.

Of one thing I am sure: we all are born, and we all must die someday. We hope death will come later rather than earlier. War is similar to disease. In the past, people died from plague and epidemics. Why did one person survive and another die? It rarely made sense. Life is a miracle and a mystery. I make a point to thank God for my death before it happens and whenever it happens. I take care of my body, live moderately, and allow love to be part of my life. These actions could give me a longer life, but they might not. In some ways, Martin Luther King Jr.'s death was a blessing in disguise in that violence and hatred were then exposed. Although every injury and death I experienced in Iraq were sad, I also received them as blessings from God.

It is important to live each day as the gift it is regardless of our surroundings. In Iraq, I occasionally slipped away for a nighttime walk between the chow hall and the hospital. At the craziest times, I was flooded with a sense of joy and well-being. I simply let these moments nurture me. I enjoyed these mysterious encounters for what they were: kisses of joy and peace.

There is much work to be done. My time in the desert is not complete. Thousands struggle to understand what happened to them or simply to heal. Healing will take a lifetime. War has always done this to us.

15 June 2005 **Guantanamo Bay, Cuba**

Such gratitude and joy fill my soul. The Lord continues to rise within me, not because of anything I do or say, but from the sheer creative force of love itself.

Guantanamo Bay's Navy priest invited me to cover the responsibilities of the island's Catholic chaplain for a few weeks. I am on active duty. I was last here on the Naval Base ten years ago during the influx of 20,000 Cuban and Haitian refugees. Terrorism detainees are now here in the same place where I previously served for three months. Many American service members and Filipino nationals work among the detainees. Numerous emotions swirl within me. I have come full circle.

During the past couple of years, I have discovered solitude. I am alone often. I am so content to be alone, although I truly love being with people. I search within my being and charge my internal battery by plugging into the source of Creation.

Today, I learned I have been passed over yet again for commander in the Naval Chaplain Corps. Like the Hebrews in Egypt, I see the "Passover" as a good thing. After twenty-eight years in the Naval and Coast Guard Reserves, it might be time to retire. Part of me thanks God for being passed over. I am not a commander, and I have no intentions of commanding in the Navy. I have been a pastor, and that is beyond my dreams. The Lord has gifted me with so much. I am rich in many things: friends, intimacy, homes, and love. I need for nothing. I am not poor. Even if all was taken from me, I believe I would still praise God and dance with the moon and stars. My faith and my minuscule vision of heaven make me a very rich and wealthy man. Thank you, Lord, Jesus. Gratitude overflows from me. Help me to be more generous and kind and loving.

You rock!

Love,

Ron Moses +

A family stationed in Guantanamo Bay, Cuba, love to take pictures. They enjoy photography immensely. The family of six (including four children) invited me to dinner on the beach and to a photo shoot at sunset. I framed this picture. (June 2005) (Father and Son)

Saint Cyprian says,

"The devil throws up obstacles to prevent our mind and our conduct

from obeying God in all things."

Last day of active duty

Praise God from whom all blessings flow!

Guantanamo Bay, Cuba

June 2005

5 July 2005 Streams of Tears

One year ago, today, I was called to go to Iraq.

When I returned from the desert, I filled in as a priest at various parishes. I was initially reluctant to share my experiences in Iraq. I thought the blood and horror might be too intense to share with entire families gathered for worship. I was also hesitant to express some of my uglier feelings of which I was ashamed, like the boredom I experienced in Iraq when the casualty flow trickled during my last two months there. However, as I shared with genuine honesty and love, people responded with amazing gratitude, concern and affirmation, an extent to which I had never before experienced. There were no lines drawn between conservative or liberal ideologies. People wanted to share in the ultimate sacrifices of our young men and women serving our country in the war zone.

This past year, I experienced honest-to-God terror in my soul and ultimate joy and sorrow, all combined. I am so grateful for life, yet I also look forward to everlasting peace through my own death.

There is such mystery in life our earthly bodies can neither comprehend nor understand. When Edward gave me the gift of his tear moments before his death, I knew at that moment I could never keep it to myself. I was called into the desert to be torn apart. And so the tear tears me apart. God allowed me to tear in two. The only way to get from earth to heaven is through the waters. When Moses brought the Israelites through the Red (Blood) Sea, the people complained, as I so often did and continue to do, although I am ashamed and saddened to admit it. Iraq is the place where Father Abraham began and where Israel was sent to 'exile' to reevaluate the mistake of placing possessions, power and pleasures before God. Whether it is the Jordan River, Red Sea, or Atlantic Ocean, the passage might be dry. The desert might be unbearably dry. Most important, however, is the moisture provided by God through His Son.

Water and blood flowed from the side of Jesus. Water and blood still flows. "Don't be afraid," Jesus says, "I am with you always until the end of time."

Time in this world and life as we know it are the Desert. God provides all we need. Trust God. Love God. Praise God. Our Father, who loves even when we don't love Him, gives us abundant peace and joy.

Healing through the Blood and Tears

Returning from forty days at Prince of Peace Abbey

1 March 2006

I have been on sabbatical at a Benedictine Monastery just outside Camp Pendleton. A week ago, the Regimental Chaplain gave me the phone number of Ami Shea. This chaplain had arranged for my travels into the city of Fallujah. I am now on a plane heading home to Atlantic Beach, Florida. One year ago, I left Fallujah, Iraq.

I called Ami Shea on Saturday afternoon. Michael, her third-grade son, answered the phone. Ami was heading to San Diego to celebrate her birthday. The call was tough for both of us. Ami's husband, Kevin, had received Communion from me just three days before his birthday, the same day as his death. He died suddenly seventeen months ago and only thirty yards away from me. At the time, I was hearing confessions and arrived on the scene as smoke was still rising. I walked with Kevin as blood dripped from his lifeless body. Now, I was inviting Ami to walk with Kevin and me through the grief, pain and spiritual blood. How little I knew about her walk these past months.

We agreed to meet on Monday morning around 9:30 a.m. I prayed for her constantly during the next two days. I had been praying for her consistently during the last seventeen months. I prayed and begged God for the appropriate words and immense compassion.

As expected, the meeting felt a little edgy and uncomfortable.

Ami called to say she would be a bit late. I hoped to meet her as she drove up the steep hill to the Abbey. She soon called and was already in front of the Church. I was in the cloister, and I came out immediately. It was a bright, sunny and crisp day. Ami was sitting on the short wall in front of the church. I breathed in. I breathed out. She is a beautiful and athletic woman and shared that she had recently run the Marine Corps marathon. I noticed both a reluctance and a desire to enter into conversation. We met in the dining hall for the retreatants. We share a love for coffee.

The conversation is confidential. Ami is a champion in helping others who suffer through the calamity of war and the death of loved ones. Ami didn't want to cry, for she was tired of it. I could relate. I was tired, too.

Ami's tears were beautiful as they swam within her eyes, unable to escape into the desert of her face. It was a profound love. Although my time with her beloved, Kevin, had been a brief and furious few days, I realized she needed to be near me, precisely because of the role I had played. This stranger revealed herself to me as a beloved and trusted friend. A profound tragedy had united us over seventeen months earlier, yet we didn't realize it at the time. How could we have known?

After our meeting, I questioned whether I had properly connected enough with Ami. I would be going home in two days. Although Ami was unsure, I had looked into her eyes and laid my hands on her precious head and offered the Sacrament of

Reconciliation. While running to Mass as the bell rang, I invited her to Ash Wednesday Mass at the Abbey. Surprisingly, she accepted.

On Wednesday morning, Ami called to say she would be bringing her daughter, Brenna, and son, Michael, with her. She took them out of school early so they could meet me. I didn't see her before running into the sacristy and putting on my robe for Mass. In my mind, her statement kept haunting me, "I am coming as fast as I can. I promised, and I will never lie to a priest."

I didn't see Ami among the crowd until just before Communion. She looked a little anxious. The last time she attended church had been a few months prior, and she had wept too much. Colonel Patrick Malay, Battalion Commander for 3-5 Marines in Fallujah, brought her to the abbey at that time, and she cried from the moment she entered the church. Patrick had broken away from work to be here this day. After all, it was Ash Wednesday. We all looked a little silly with the ashes on our foreheads.

Ami and her daughter were standing next to each other. When my eyes finally met Ami's, I smiled, and she smiled back. It was that same kind of relief one feels after seeing a familiar face among strangers. After Mass, I learned Michael had sat with Patrick, while Ami and Brenna stood in the back of the packed church. Michael was to receive First Communion on April 22. Ami knew she needed to come home, just as her beloved Kevin did.

There are no adequate words to express the glow and radiance that washed over Ami that glorious morning. Something happened.

It was almost as if she prayed to Jesus and said, “Too heavy.” And Jesus immediately reduced the burden. Her children and I hit it off immediately. I enjoyed playing with them and flipping them over. Brother Mario’s love and compassion were touching. While Ami, Patrick and I met in a visitor’s room, he had befriended the children and provided them with lunch and entertainment, unbeknownst to us.

Patrick Malay requested a blessing for Ami and one for his recent engagement to a beautiful woman. I invoked the name of Jesus and asked that Kevin be among us. Unsolicited, Ami later said she felt Kevin walk into the room. Love ***is*** stronger than death. I brought the family into the church for a tour, and we touched all the Stations of the Cross. “Second Fall” was the most meaningful to Ami. It must be a defining characteristic of the human condition that we often slip or get stuck in the journey of life.

The Eucharist brought Kevin and me together, and it is Eucharist that will heal the gaping wound in Ami and her children as we unite in love. Loving the people I serve and ministering to them intimately bonds me to their families and to this family in particular. Love, although wonderful, hurts a lot.

The option of not loving is hell. Love heals.

The tears of Ami danced yesterday. Kevin just graced his family and me with another **Tear in the Desert.**

Love you Jesus,

Ron Moses +

2 March 2006

Landing in Atlanta

Coming Home Again!

Coming Home!

It is Finished!

(Conclusion)

Truth rests within every soul. There are many processes and religions that go about this "awakening" within ourselves. We all pretty much recognize evil when we experience it. It isn't a matter of Islam or Christianity or Judaism or Atheism or Hinduism or whatever. It is a matter of the beauty of a human being, the depth of a soul, and the mystery of the human spirit. The war is within. It isn't political, although it often masquerades behind the political, capitalist, or communist machines of man's creation.

Whenever a broken, hurting, dying or dead man, woman or child arrived in Bravo Surgical, our duties were to offer medical, compassionate, and loving services. We all bleed…spiritually, physically, emotionally, and psychologically. When will we ever learn this? We are all created for so much more. We are all created in the image of something so different and not found in Nature. Is it possible all human beings were created in order to become divine? The potential we all have for **love** is what binds us together. In our infancy, we reach for the love of a mother and a father. Nothing else suffices. We even pursue this basic love when our lifestyles, religion and choices seem to contradict this desire to live and rest in love.

All people ARE created equal. Tears will continue to flow in the desert until the thirst is quenched. After Jesus was nailed on the cross, he made just seven statements. His profound words contradicted all revenge and bitterness. He truly is the God I worship. Utter love. He spoke words of love and concern for the people he came to love and bring home. No longer does God send us alone. God takes us.

"Father, forgive them; they know not what they do."

"Today you will be with me in Paradise."

"Woman, behold your son. Son, behold your mother."

"My God, My God, why have you abandoned me?"

"Father, into your hands I commend my spirit."

"It is finished."

Afterward by Colonel Michael Shupp, USMC

At the beginning of November 2004, the First Marine Expeditionary Force began the largest urban assault of a city since the Korean War. Over six Brigade equivalents, roughly 20,000 Marines, Sailors, Soldiers and Airmen of the Joint, Coalition and Partner Nations began the attack on the terrorist stronghold of Fallujah. During this period, I commanded Regimental Combat Team-1, the Main Effort of the ground attack. Our mission was to attack Fallujah, eliminate terrorist forces and return the City to the legitimate Government of Iraq.

Over the course of nine months of fighting prior to the attack on Fallujah, our Regimental Combat Team was subjected to artillery fire, improvised explosive device attacks and regular small arms ambushes by enemy forces operating from City. The enemy had created a strongpoint or base of operations and the Coalition was prevented from entering the City. From the sand bag bunkers of Traffic Control Point–1 on the East side of the City, we faced daily attacks against our forces locked in a standoff across a no man's land of urban rubble. Fallujah had become a center of enemy activity that enabled them to plan, organize, and attack throughout Iraq.

Upon assuming command of RCT-1, I first met Chaplain Ron Camarda at church services. The Regiment was stationed about 45 minutes outside of the City of Fallujah in an old Iraqi Military

Base. Coming from the conservative Catholic Church of the Northeast United States and the military, I was taken off guard by this enthusiastic Chaplain who brought music, every verse of every hymn, and a strong voice to our services. Sunday services were Chaplain Camarda's time to allow all of us, regardless of rank, to escape our tremendous responsibilities. He did this by forcing us to relax, sing and reflect on the strength of our Faith. I've got to admit, he was out of place and all of us needed a quick service to permit us to get back to our duties, but in reflection our Chaplain Camarda was caring for our emotional and long term well being. Each Sunday, my encounters with Chaplain Camarda were limited to my wonderful Sergeant Major Leardo and I attending services. Although our encounters were brief, Chaplain Camarda provided each of us a medal or cross to keep with us. I received an olive cross that fit nicely in my uniform cargo pocket right next to my heart. In the course of nine months of fighting and under the weight of my body armor, this cross would wrap around my body and still retains the shape of those challenging times.

As the prepatory attacks occurred against Fallujah prior to the assault, I again encountered Chaplain Camarda at the Bravo Surgical Hospital aboard Camp Fallujah. Bravo Surgical was the first medical evacuation point with surgical capabilities for our forces. Here these brilliant Navy Doctors, Nurses and Corpsmen earned the title, "Cheaters of Death" as they beat impossible odds to heal our gallant warriors. When the fighting would finish, this was always one of my first stops to visit where Sergeant Major

Leardo and I could ensure for the care of our wounded. Entering the chaotic receiving area of Bravo Surgical, I found Chaplain Camarda comforting the wounded and caring for the survivors of the fighting. I would later find out that he also was the Chaplain of the Surgical Hospital. We could not have been luckier.

At this point, he became Father Ron and not just another Chaplain. As I looked into the surgical rooms, I could see him talking to the wounded and caring for them as if they were his children. It didn't matter their faith or denomination, Father Ron was there to breathe in life or to help our Angels pass with comfort, dignity and respect. Father Ron did this with song, words of prayer or by holding on to us as we were ripped apart by the violence of war. I will never forget him for caring for our warriors. I can't think of a more difficult assignment, but we were blessed with the right man – Father Ron Camarda!

But his service didn't stop there. About one week into the battle as we began the desperate house to house clearing operations, I walked out of our forward headquarters in downtown Fallujah to see Father Ron just arriving with a resupply convoy. With the fighting occurring all around us, he had come to provide us Sunday services. When I first saw him, I was overcome with his commitment to each of us. Here was a Catholic Priest, who put our welfare first regardless of the desperate fighting. Unfortunately, I told him that I didn't have time for services as I was moving forward into the fight, but he offered the blessed sacrament of our faith. So in downtown Fallujah amidst the rubble of battle and as I was preparing to move forward, Father Ron provided my fighting team the strength of our faith to continue with our mission to help the people of Iraq. Each Sunday, Father Ron became a regular and would make the difficult journey to provide us services. Some of my fondest memories were of his services in those forward positions. I will never forget the strength of our voices at the Christmas services.

After six months of fighting, Coalition forces cleared the City of Fallujah of enemy forces and enabled the Government of Iraq to enter the City. It is estimated that our forces killed approximately 2,000 enemy fighters and captured a like amount. With the City secured, we enabled the return of the citizens, reconstructed the City and enabled the first free Iraqi election with the largest recorded vote in Al Anbar province. Fallujah would become what many would call the safest place in Iraq. On one occasion while escorting the Multi- National Corps Operations Officer, a United Kingdom General, he remarked that he had never seen finer forces in the field. He complimented the Regimental Combat Team on its ability to conduct desperate fighting and no more than a short distance away simultaneously provide humanitarian assistance to the Iraqi Citizens. As I reflected on his comments, I realized that our strength came from our professional training, but also from the Moral Courage that had been developed in each of us.

Father Ron Camarda is one of those quiet heroes, who made a difference in so many ways. Through his enthusiasm and compassion, he strengthened and developed our moral courage to face the horrors of war. When injured physically or emotionally, his strength and commitment held us up to face each day with dignity and courage. I will never forget him or his service to the Regiment. God is Good, All the Time!

Semper Fi

Col Mike Shupp

Inchon 6 Commander Officer,

Regimental Combat Team-1, Fallujah 2004-2005

TEARS STILL IN THE DESERT

(After the Rain)

April clutched the green notebook bound together by threads and heavy black tape. The notebook had traveled with me to Iraq and back. Many of the pages were soiled and smudged. Some were marked with coffee, sweat, oils of the body and even blood. My finger had often reached up and brushed my cheek and then returned to the pages…a tear or two or three…

April leafed through this shattered notebook that contained over two thousand names buried within its pages. I gently guided her to the page where I had written the name of her beloved husband. He had been shot and eventually died in my presence over two years ago as I held his hand and heart.

The name of April's husband had appeared on the front page of the Florida Times Union newspaper fourteen months earlier. With modern global and information accessibility, this article has literally spread across the world. Her husband's name, along with a little cross, has been seen by millions, yet very few realize what that name means to April… maybe no one knows but April.

As April pondered this reality in her hands, there was an awkward silence. Maybe she had expected my visit to squelch the fires of her need to know all of the facts surrounding her husband's death.

April questioned and probed me in her desire to understand if she could continue this relationship of love with Shane who had been killed in action. Not only did Shane die, but part of April died. Will it ever be known?

The papers and media in Omaha concentrated on the fact that April gave birth to their only begotten son at the same hour of Shane's death. Indeed, this seems newsworthy and profound. Even I put too much emphasis on this detail, which is both an overwhelming tragedy and blessing.

How would Shane's death have been reported by the media had April not been pregnant? How many widows are not singled out because of a lack of this sort of "miracle"? Over four thousand military deaths have occurred since this war began. April suffered through the death of her beloved who also happens to be the father of her son. April will forever greet each day with this horror of loss and a plethora of never-ending questions. As a nation, how can we cope with so much emptiness, loss and confusion?

As April held my journal, it seemed as if I was giving part of myself away. Her eyes met mine, and our tears flowed. I will never know what happened within her soul as we embraced. The tears washed over us.

Composure returned swiftly. The encounter was profound.

I am still in contact with April. She has found a lasting peace that was missing for some time. I can only imagine the depth of courage it must take to be the face of so much hidden pain. April wrote:

Meeting you was such an amazing joy and I can't tell you the last time I have felt completely at "peace" after leaving you. You are such an amazing man and will forever be in my heart and prayers.

It is a good thing to be prayed for by modern-day saints like April. Stories of others are difficult for me to process without reliving my own pain and traumatic stress. War is a nasty thing. It scars not only those who witness the horror on the front lines, but leaves millions more struggling to trudge through the spiritual and emotional carnage.

We need each other not only to find clarity. We need each other for the love that is lacking in this world. I see love. I really see love in the eyes of the mourning. I am grateful the few moments I have spent with so many have produced more love and not hatred or bitterness.

Love is a choice, not a feeling.

Love can free us and heal us if we have the courage to forgive like Jesus.

Ron Moses Camarda +

May 27th 2007, Memorial Day Weekend

My Space with April Kielion

www.myspace.com

April **April 5th, 2007** **7:14 AM**

Hey baby, I have such wonderful news!!!

I have been emailing Fr Ron Camarda and we are going to meet him next Tuesday! I am so excited. I know Our Lord works in mysterious ways and to meet the man who was with you for your last moments is truly a blessing for me. I know the emotions will be completely overwhelming but I know I need to do this. I know you will be there with us too! Help give me the strength to not "lose it" in front of our son and keep me composed a little! I miss you more than you could ever know my love, xoxoxoxo, April.

April **April 11, 2007** **5:49 AM**

Wow, is all I have to say about Father Ron---what an amazing man! I feel at peace for the first time in 2 years and 4 months --- I have all of my questions answered and know that you are truly in the arms of Our Lord. I feel blessed to know that Father was with you and you were not alone. I only wish that I could have been there but I know you would have never wanted me to see you that way. You know, denial is an amazing thing baby. I lived in a sheer fog for well over a year and truly believed that you were still deployed. Finally my head and heart agreed that that was not the case and I know the truth. Last night that truth was made very blatantly obvious to me when Father Ron described 3 of your tattoos on your chest. I thought I was going to lose it but it is as if you were there giving me the strength to hold it together. Thank you my love. You are such a strong individual and I miss you more and more every day. Come visit me in my dreams baby! I love you, your angel, xoxoxo

August 4, 2007

Father Ron's Comments:

This is truly a story that keeps on going. That day that I prayed and was present when Shane died is truly bigger than the few breaths that I experienced. There was a permanent tattoo placed on my heart. It cannot be erased.

This is how Sacraments work. When we are baptized in the Name of the Father and of the Son and of the Holy Spirit, we are more than tattooed on the heart or the soul. We are more than branded as Children of God. We become part of a very special family forever. This is mind boggling. This is great news. So when I anointed this man, it was forever. I forgave his sins. I traced the Oils of the Church on his bloody forehead and body. This movement, this action must have been excruciatingly painful, more painful than the bullet that caused his death, for Shane and his family and friends. And yet, it is bonded like two wax candles melted and then formed into one; impossible to separate. "Through this holy anointing, may the Lord in his love and mercy help you through the grace of the Holy Spirit." And then after tracing the oil on his head in the form of a cross, I traced the cross on his hands and body saying, "May the Lord who frees you from sin, save you and raise you up."

Shane was healed in those few moments before he died. I believe this with my whole being. And then just exactly two years and five months, in the same manner and in the hotel lobby, I anointed Shane's wife, April, who gave birth to their son at the same hour of his death. April was healed at that moment. Yes, the pain is still there, and the grieving will continue but she was healed deeply, physically, emotionally and spiritually. God is always faithful to His promises.

And so, we continue to journey in faith.

What a true gift this family is to our Church. What a blessing.

Let us be filled with gratitude.

Amen.

Shane and April Kielion

Shane E. Kielion, Jr.

Born November 15, 2004

Friend of Edward Iwan

I received the following e-mail in September 2007:

Father Ron,

Sir, I'm a long a go friend of Edward Iwan's and I recently read an article by Mark Woods on you and Ed's last moments. Ed and I were friends at the University of Nebraska where I was going to graduate school in philosophy and Ed was an undergraduate. Ed befriended me and took me out shooting at the National Guard Armory to help me with my marksmanship. I eventually shot perfectly on the M16 test under Ed's tutorship. Ed would go out of his way to help those around him; he truly cared about his troops. I read about how Ed died in several accounts on-line; all reflect the Ed that I remember. He was wounded in his Bradley Fighting Vehicle by a rocket propelled grenade in the abdomen. Ed kept quiet after being fatally injured, I believe, to keep his troops from panicking and creating more casualties. His troops revered him and recognized his ability to lead, his experience, his quick decision making, and his passion for his troops' well-being. I hope that in my military career I'll be able to resemble his leadership. But more than anything I want to thank you for being there for Ed when he died. Your words of comfort in Ed's time of need were echoed in the minds of all that knew him and loved him. His parents and friends would have screamed out in all their power "Ed, I love you!" to ease his passing from this world to God's heaven; and I thank you for being that voice for all of us. There are many at the University of Nebraska who knew and loved Ed as a friend and your actions at his side when he needed God most are appreciated and not forgotten. Thank you and God bless you.

Very Respectfully,

Capt Ron Hustwit, Jr. USAF
Beale AFB, CA

Gratitude to Edward Iwan from Father Ron

12 November 2007

Three years ago today, I held a man, figuratively and literally, as he died. He was stretched out in the operating room like a crucified man, on his back, guts hanging out. I had overwhelming love for this man whom I had just met. I was exhausted from the war, embattled, depressed, belittled and frustrated.

And yet I could see in the dark murky moments... a sense of light. Edward opened me up to a world I never knew existed. The tear, which gently and remarkably escaped his closed eye, was a prism of light that flooded my soul.

Honestly, I still can't find the words, thoughts, or song to express what happened, nor what is continually happening to my being. It seems to be a good thing, but I can never be totally sure.

As soon as this moment of love, joy and sorrow broke into that operating room in Fallujah, Iraq... it seemed to slip out in a vanquished moment. How did I get there? Where did part of me go? I also left the room, and I continue to wait for the return of my mind? my spirit? my soul?

Part of me was killed in action without a trace. My friends and family still look into my eyes and search for the Ron who has yet to return home, and may never return. Although I often emit a sense of apathy, I sense something is left undone, unfinished.

Edward, the corpsman, the nurse and I are still confined in that cramped little operating room that may no longer even physically exist. But it is there for me. Like a crime scene, the evidence of the destructive force of war and violence is waiting to be discovered and solved, or at least, to be compassionately closed and sealed forever.

Thank you, Edward, on the anniversary of your death and resurrection, for coursing through my eyes, my writing, my blood and my soul.

I love you. Go with God and with Jesus.

You have nothing to fear.

Love: a wonderful joy,

Peace, joy, love,

Ron Moses +

Gratitude

I would like to thank the following for their part in this story:

My Beloved Father in Heaven and on Earth

The men and women who sacrificed their lives for our freedoms and who inspired me to pray for them and love them as my own sons and daughters

The men and women who sacrificed their limbs, psyches, and time with their families for our freedoms (I wonder if the Purple Heart should be awarded to those who are diagnosed with PTSD?)

For relatives and friends who experienced the death of their beloved in this war. Especially parents, children and spouses

The Marines, Soldiers, Airmen, and Sailors with whom I had the honor of serving

My Parents, Matthew and Margaret, for giving me life and instilling faith, family, love and fun into my life (And for my new mother, Momma Nancy who loves me as a son)

My Brothers: Ray, Steve, Gerry, Rick, and Andy for so many ways you were there through this ordeal.

My Sisters: Diane, Susan, and PJ for so many prayers and tears, along with putting up with the chore of being sisters to a priest. Diane made stoles for all 24 who received Sacraments in the Desert.

For the sisters by marriage: Diane, Martha, Mary, and Ami for being my sisters and always leaving the door open for me.

Father Jeff McGowan for being my beloved friend and spiritual partner into the desert and enriching my life in our journeys

Sister Patricia O'Hea for being my other beloved friend through thick and thin

Sister Carmel and all the Sisters of Mercy (and Rebecca)

The People of Saint Patrick's in North Jacksonville for the computer I took into the battle and used for various liturgies and in which I wrote the bulk of this book. Also for supporting me with so much love that I had plenty to share in the field.

Bishop John Snyder for ordaining me, inspiring me, and having faith in me.

Father Richard Grasso who is a second father to me

Bishop Victor Galeone for trusting me to represent the Diocese of St. Augustine and to reflect an abundance of Love, Joy and Peace!

The Knights of Columbus for the thousands of religious medals

Those who sent me so many gifts of prayers, love, care packages and love

John and Nancy Kearney (Matthew & Kyle) for greeting me at Camp Pendleton as their own brother and uncle

Stan and Kate Norton (kids and dogs) for your incredible generosity and love; Kate was the first editor of my manuscript. She told me the story needed to get out. The DVD Stan produced for my retirement inspired me to keep going, have faith and have fun in the process.

RP1 Patrick Bowen for saving my life (literally) more than once and for making our Ministry Team the Best! (You really should be a Senior Chief!)

Colonel Michael Shupp for the Afterward and for trusting me with your Marines (and his wife, Sherrye who continues to live!)

The people behind the names and faces who appear in these pages

Mark Woods and Marc Hardesty for lighting a fire under my…heart!

The People of the Diocese of St. Augustine

Curtis Loftis for his artistic flair in the cover concept and design

My grass roots editors: Anne Wall and Maria Lee Richburg;
Maria Lee (Scott, her husband, and five daughters) lovingly edited the story and nurtured Tear in the Desert to its full potential.

Susi Pittman (+Greg) for her unwavering, generous and passionate support of this story and ministry. Your star is brightly shining!

Those of you who have enriched the story, especially those who grieve the losses of life, limb and love in this war

Jesus and the Holy Spirit

A U.S. Marine with Company K, 3rd Battalion, 1st Marine Regiment, kneels in front of a memorial staged in Camp Abu Ghurab, Iraq, to remember four of their fallen, Sgt. Christopher T. Heflin, Sgt. Morgan W. Strader, Lance Cpl. Jeremy A. Ailes and Lance Cpl. Juan E. Segura Dec. 27. On November 9 I wrote in my green journal:

+Juan Eduardo Segura
LCPL May 28 B.
Anoint Catholic – (Apostolic Pardon)
2 Rosaries – Our Lady of Guadalupe

This is the exact place where I experienced the "Memorial Service" for seven Marines from Company L, 3-1 Marines, 20 January 2005.

"Behold, I am with you always until the end of time!"

- Jesus

Printed in the United States
154024LV00002B/22/P

9 780615 195780